FEARLESS FELINES

30

TRUE TALES OF

COURAGEOUS
CATS

FOR SCOUT, SAMMY JO, ELSA, AND WHISKERS. FOUR VERY FINE CATS INDEED.

Text copyright © 2019 by Kimberlie Hamilton
Illustrations copyright © 2019 by Allie Runnion, Andrew Gardner, Becky Davies,
Charlotte Archer, Emma Jayne, Holly Sterling, Hui Skipp, Jessica Smith, Katie Wilson,
Lily Rossiter, Michelle Hird, Nan Lawson, Olivia Holden, Rachel Allsop, Rachel Sanson, Sam Loman

Library of Congress Cataloging-in-Publication Data

Names: Hamilton, Kimberlie, author. | Runnion, Allie, illustrator.
Title: Fearless felines : 30 true tales of courageous cats /
    Kimberlie Hamilton ; illustrations by Allie Runnion, Andrew Gardner,
    Becky Davies, Charlotte Archer, Emma Jayne, Bonnie Pang, Holly Sterling,
    Hui Skipp, Jessica Smith, Katie Wilson, Lily Rossiter, Michelle Hird,
    Nan Lawson, Olivia Holden, Rachel Allsop, Rachel Sanson and Sam Loman.
Description: New York, NY : Scholastic Press, [2019] | Includes index. |
    Audience: Age 8-12.
Identifiers: LCCN 2018060123 | ISBN 9781338355833 (paper over board : alk. paper)
Subjects: LCSH: Cats—Anecdotes—Juvenile literature.
Classification: LCC SF445.7 .H3617 2019 | DDC 636.8--dc23
LC record available at https://catalog.loc.gov/vwebv/search?search
    Code=LCCN&searchArg=2018060123&searchType=1&permalink=y

10 9 8 7 6 5 4 3 2 1   19 20 21 22 23

Printed in Malaysia 108
First edition November 2019

FEARLESS FELINES

30

TRUE TALES OF

COURAGEOUS CATS

KIMBERLIE HAMILTON

ILLUSTRATIONS BY

ALLIE RUNNION, ANDREW GARDNER, BECKY DAVIES, CHARLOTTE ARCHER, EMMA JAYNE, HOLLY STERLING, HUI SKIPP, JESSICA SMITH, KATIE WILSON, LILY ROSSITER, MICHELLE HIRD, NAN LAWSON, OLIVIA HOLDEN, RACHEL ALLSOP, RACHEL SANSON, BONNIE PANG, AND SAM LOMAN

■ SCHOLASTIC

CONTENTS

CATS CAN BE HEROES, TOO!

Cats are adventurers and born survivors. Many have led incredible, inspiring, and interesting lives, yet have been forgotten or overlooked by history. Not fair, right?

This book will set the record straight with tales of more than thirty real-life kitties that are the heroes of their own stories.

You'll find out about World War II legends, fearless sailors on the high seas, Guinness World Record holders, cats that inspired bestsellers, and many more—even an "astro-cat" that traveled to space (and made it back to Earth to tell the tale).

Ready? Get set for some remarkable feline facts and fur-raising adventures!

WHAT HAPPENED WHEN

7500 BC
FIRST PET CAT IS BURIED ALONGSIDE ITS HUMAN. TOGETHER FUR-EVER!

1233
POPE GREGORY IX SAYS CATS COULD BE THE DEVIL IN DISGUISE.

800
AN ANONYMOUS IRISH MONK WRITES A POEM ABOUT HIS CAT, PANGUR BÁN.

980 BC
GREEK AND PHOENICIAN TRADERS BRING CATS TO EUROPE.

1492
CATS ABOARD COLUMBUS'S SHIPS REACH THE AMERICAS.

55 BC
CATS COME TO BRITAIN WITH INVADING ROMANS.

500 BC
THE CHINESE EMPEROR RECEIVES A KITTY AS A GIFT.

1348
CATS ARE BLAMED FOR SPREADING THE BLACK DEATH. (NOT TRUE!)

1000
RATS, RATS, RATS! CATS ARE IN HOT DEMAND IN INCREASINGLY OVERCROWDED CITIES.

4000 BC
CATS IN ANCIENT EGYPT ARE TREATED LIKE GODS.

1600s
NEWS FLASH: CATS WEREN'T TO BLAME FOR THE PLAGUE! OOPS.

600
THE PROPHET MUHAMMAD ENCOURAGES HIS FOLLOWERS TO BE KIND TO CATS.

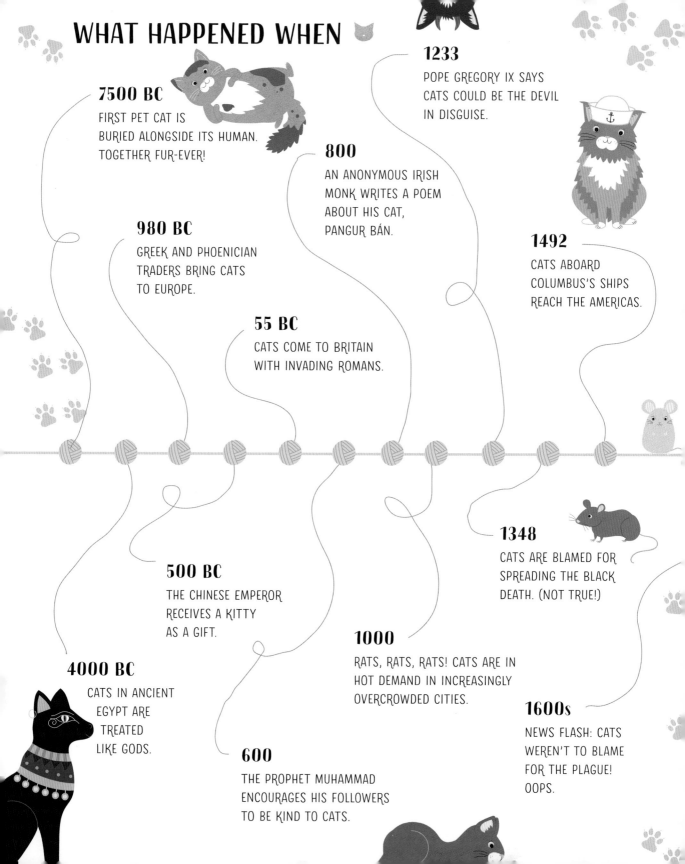

1914

CATS SERVE IN THE TRENCHES OF WORLD WAR I.

2018

500 MILLION (AND COUNTING) CATS LIVE AROUND THE WORLD. SPAYING AND NEUTERING CATS IS MORE IMPORTANT THAN EVER.

1606

SHAKESPEARE'S PLAYS MENTION CATS MORE THAN FORTY TIMES BUT RARELY IN A NICE WAY.

1966

THE ANIMAL WELFARE ACT BECOMES LAW IN THE UNITED STATES.

1871

THE WORLD'S FIRST CAT SHOW, HELD AT THE CRYSTAL PALACE IN LONDON.

2001

THE WORLD'S FIRST CLONED PET IS BORN, A CAT NAMED CC (SHORT FOR "COPY CAT").

1995

PET CATS OUTNUMBER DOGS FOR THE FIRST TIME IN THE UNITED STATES. THE UNITED KINGDOM IS CLOSE BEHIND.

1911

BRITAIN PASSES THE PROTECTION OF ANIMALS ACT.

1692

THE SALEM WITCH TRIALS IN AMERICA. BAD NEWS FOR CATS.

1939

WORLD WAR II STARTS. CATS DO THEIR PART FOR THE WAR EFFORT.

2006

NEW LAWS IN THE US SAY THAT PETS MUST BE RESCUED WITH THEIR OWNERS DURING DISASTERS. THE UK PASSES THE ANIMAL WELFARE ACT, WHICH MAKES IT ILLEGAL TO HARM CATS.

FEARLESS
FELINES!

BEERBOHM
SCENE-STEALING THEATER CAT

There once was a time when every theater had its very own cat. Theater cats hunted mice and were said to bring good luck—especially black cats. Some actors even smuggled their own black kitties backstage to make sure they had a successful show!

The most famous theater cat was a stocky tabby named Beerbohm. He spent almost twenty years of his long life at what is now known as the Gielgud Theatre in London's West End.

Beerbohm liked to play favorites with certain actors. He'd shower them with attention, twirling around their ankles and napping in their dressing rooms. And at least once during every show's run, he would stroll onstage right in the middle of a performance! With an oddball name like Beerbohm, he was a cat destined to be in the spotlight.

Like many cats, Beerbohm could be a little naughty. He once chewed the feathers off some hats in the costume room. Another time, he ripped apart a collection of stuffed birds in the prop closet. But his worst offense? That would be the time he used a sand-covered stage as a giant litter box. The audience loved it. The actors, not so much.

Beerbohm's best buddy was Fleur, the kitty at the theater next door. He often went to visit her, dodging London's black cabs and red double-decker buses to get there.

This theatrical pussycat retired to the countryside, where he lived a drama-free life with one of the theater's carpenters. You can still see a portrait of him today, displayed in a place of honor in the lobby of the Gielgud.

1975–1995
ENGLAND

SILLY CAT SUPERSTITIONS

As **BEERBOHM** knew all too well, theater people can be super superstitious about anything that might mess up a performance. For example, few actors ever say *"MACBETH"* inside a theater—they call it **"THE SCOTTISH PLAY."** Whistling in a theater is also a big no-no, and you should **NEVER** wish an actor **"GOOD LUCK."** Tell them to **"BREAK A LEG"** instead!

There seem to be more superstitions about cats than any other animal—especially black cats. Here are a few cat superstitions **(ALL NONSENSE, OF COURSE):**

- IF A CAT GROOMS ITSELF, GUESTS ARE COMING.

- A SNEEZING KITTY IS GOOD LUCK.

- A WOMAN WITH A BLACK CAT WILL HAVE NO TROUBLE FINDING A HUSBAND.

- A CAT CROSSING YOUR PATH IS BAD LUCK OR GOOD LUCK, DEPENDING ON WHERE YOU LIVE.

- PUT A CAT WHISKER IN YOUR WALLET TO ATTRACT MONEY.

- IF YOU PAY FOR A CAT WITH MONEY, IT WILL NEVER BE A GOOD MOUSER.

- FINDING A WHITE HAIR ON A BLACK CAT IS GOOD LUCK.

- A CAT BROUGHT INTO A NEW HOME THROUGH THE WINDOW WILL NEVER RUN AWAY.

- A TRI-COLORED CAT WILL PROTECT YOU FROM FEVERS AND FIRES.

BOB
A STREET CAT GONE HOLLYWOOD

One cold night in London, a down-on-his-luck street musician named James found an injured and hungry tomcat. He gave him some food and took him to a vet, spending what little money he had on some medication for the poor kitty. He named the friendly orange cat Bob.

Bob didn't move on once his injuries healed. He went wherever James went. He rode around on James's shoulder and even traveled with him on buses and the London Underground. While James played his guitar and sang on street corners, Bob sat on the guitar case and calmly watched the world go by. Sometimes he'd "high-five" James with his paw, which always made onlookers smile.

Commuters began to stop by just to talk to Bob and take his picture. They posted videos and photos of the pair online. A literary agent saw the posts and thought the heart-warming story might make a good book.

She was right. *A Street Cat Named Bob* became an instant bestseller in countries around the world. James then went on to write more books about his beloved cat.

But this wasn't the peak of Bob's feline fame. That came when *A Street Cat Named Bob* was turned into a Hollywood film! The film director's original plan was to use "Bob-alikes"—six specially trained cat actors—but Bob had other ideas. He stole the show during the filming of one scene, and from then on, he played himself as often as possible.

At the film's red-carpet premiere, Bob was introduced to a royal fan—Kate Middleton, the Duchess of Cambridge. Not bad for a cat who used to be homeless!

BORN C. 2007
ENGLAND

HOW TO TELL IF A CAT LOVES YOU

Cats are known for being loners, but are they really the cold creatures they're sometimes made out to be? Many cats form close bonds with their humans, just like **BOB** did. Here are a few ways cats can show they care:

- **PURRING** IS A RUMBLING SOUND A CAT MAKES WHEN THEY'RE RELAXED AND HAPPY.

- **ROLLING ON THE GROUND** BELLY-UP MEANS A CAT TRUSTS YOU.

- **BUNTING** IS WHEN A CAT RUBS ITS CHEEKS OR HEAD ON YOU.

- **KNEADING YOUR LAP** IS SOMETHING A CAT DOES WHEN IT'S FEELING CONTENT.

- 🐾 **SLEEPING ON YOUR LAP** OR BED IS A SIGN THAT A CAT FEELS COMFORTABLE.

- 🐾 **SLOW EYE BLINKS** ARE A KITTY "KISS." GIVE A SLOW BLINK BACK!

- 🐾 **UPRIGHT TAILS** MEAN "I'M HAPPY TO SEE YOU!" THE SAME GOES FOR A CAT'S BOTTOM IN YOUR FACE.

- 🐾 **MEOWING** IS SOMETHING A CAT WILL ONLY DO WHEN IT WANTS TO "TALK" TO A HUMAN. CATS TEND NOT TO MEOW AT OTHER CATS.

- 🐾 **LICKING YOUR SKIN** OR NIBBLING YOUR HAIR IS ANOTHER CUTE DISPLAY OF AFFECTION.

- 🐾 **GIFTING A DEAD INSECT OR MOUSE** IS A CAT'S WAY OF SAYING "I LOVE YOU." (CATS KNOW HUMANS ARE FAR TOO CLUELESS TO CATCH SUCH A DELICIOUS TREAT ON THEIR OWN!)

COLIN'S
NEW ZEALAND STOWAWAY

Colin's was the resident pussycat at the Port Taranaki tanker terminal in New Zealand. Everyone called her Colin's Cat (or just Colin's), after the man who found her.

Colin's used every trick in the book to get people to feed her. One day, she charmed a crew member on a large tanker known as the *Tomiwaka* into taking her on board for a snack. They fell asleep in his cabin, and when they woke up, the ship was headed to South Korea!

When the ship's captain learned of the furry stowaway, he let everyone back in New Zealand know that Colin's was safe. She wasn't exactly going hungry, either. The Kiwi kitty had the crew feeding her bites of salmon, beef, and chips.

But how was Colin's to get home? The *Tomiwaka* wasn't going back to New Zealand, and a ship-to-ship transfer would be too risky. The only option was to keep her on board for the 6,200-mile voyage and figure it out once they made it to South Korea.

By this time, Colin's adventure was international news. An airline offered to fly Port Taranaki's head honcho to South Korea to fetch the cat. When the *Tomiwaka* finally reached land, four camera crews were on hand to record the happy reunion.

Colin's bid farewell to the tanker crew and the pair flew home to New Zealand. A big crowd gathered at the airport to greet her, and the mayor even gave her a special medal. Best of all, a cat-food company gave the intrepid feline a lifetime supply of cat food.

Colin's never again strayed far from Port Taranaki, which henceforth called itself the "Home of Colin's Cat."

1991–2007
NEW ZEALAND

CATS AHOY!

Cats like **COLIN'S** have traveled on ships since ancient times. Over the centuries, ship cats became such a tradition that many sailors wouldn't board a vessel without one!

CATS AND THE WEATHER

Ship folklore says that cats can predict the weather. But is that really true? The answer is . . . **MAYBE**. A cat can often sense changes in the weather well before a human can. Keep an eye on your kitty to see if any of these old sayings are the real deal:

- IF A CAT SNEEZES, **RAIN** IS ON THE WAY.
- A CAT SLEEPING WITH ALL FOUR PAWS TUCKED UNDER MEANS **COLD WEATHER**.
- IF A CAT YAWNS AND STRETCHES OUT, IT MEANS **NICE WEATHER**.
- A CAT ACTING PLAYFUL MEANS THE **WIND** WILL PICK UP.
- A LOUDLY MEOWING CAT MEANS A **DIFFICULT VOYAGE** AHEAD.
- THROWING A CAT OVERBOARD WILL CAUSE A TERRIBLE **STORM!**

FAMOUS SHIP CATS

BLACKIE became a celebrity when Sir Winston Churchill came aboard his Royal Navy ship and gave him a friendly pat. The cat's name was changed to Churchill soon after.

CONVOY of the HMS *Hermione* received the same uniform as every other sailor, including a teeny-tiny hammock to sleep in.

PEEBLES served on the HMS *Western Isles* during World War II. He loved to perform tricks for the crew, such as jumping through hoops.

TIDDLES was the mouser on several Royal Navy aircraft carriers. He's one reason why black cats are often considered good luck in Great Britain.

DID YOU KNOW?
A SAILOR'S WIFE OFTEN KEPT A BLACK CAT IN THE HOUSE TO ENSURE HER HUSBAND'S SAFE RETURN.

CSALOGÁNY
BELOVED BARNYARD BUDDY

The legendary Hungarian racehorse Kincsem never lost a race and is considered one of the greatest thoroughbreds of all time. Yet few people know that the secret to her success may have been her closest friend,
a cat named Csalogány.

Racehorses, like all horses, are pack animals and can get skittish and anxious. They often take comfort from having a little buddy to hang out with, like a pony or a goat. It helps keep them calm and relaxed before and after a race. But a companion cat? That's pretty rare, even for a horse as quirky and unique as Kincsem.

Csalogány means "nightingale" in Hungarian, although no one can remember exactly why she was named this. What hasn't been forgotten is that Csalogány and Kincsem were absolutely inseparable. They even traveled all over Europe together, going from one racetrack to the next.

After one race, Csalogány and her long-legged equine friend went by ship across the English Channel to France. Kincsem eagerly clip-clopped her way down the gangplank to dry land, but the cat was nowhere to be found. The distraught filly refused to board her railway car until Csalogány joined her. She stood on the pier for two solid hours, feet firmly planted and ears pinned back. She wasn't going anywhere without that cat.

Csalogány finally scampered off the ship and ran over to Kincsem. The horse tossed her head and greeted the cat with a loud and joyful whinny. "*Neighhhh*-ver do that again!" she seemed to say. Csalogány hopped up onto the filly's back and the reunited pair happily headed off on another adventure.

After all, life is always better with your best friend by your side!

C. 1874–UNKNOWN
HUNGARY

DEWEY
THE WORLD'S MOST FAMOUS LIBRARY CAT

On a freezing January night, somebody with a heart of stone stuffed a tiny kitten into the library drop box of Spencer, Iowa, a small Midwestern town. The staff found him the next morning and decided to keep him. They named him Dewey, after the Dewey Decimal System used for sorting books. It was the perfect name for a library cat!

Dewey took to his new role with gusto. He greeted patrons and snuggled in their laps. He rode around on the book cart and purred next to children while they had stories read to them. He napped on top of the computers and played hide-and-seek in the bookshelves. The staff kept a camera handy to record his hilarious antics.

Stories about Dewey began to appear in magazines and newspapers. He became the January cat on a nationwide calendar. He was featured on TV and in a video about library cats. A documentary team even came all the way from Tokyo to film him. People drove hundreds of miles out of their way just to meet the little orange cat.

While everyone loved Dewey, the person who loved him the most was his caretaker, the library's director. She wrote a bestselling book called *Dewey: The Small-Town Library Cat Who Touched the World*. The cat from America's heartland did indeed have fans around the globe. But his biggest fans were the local townspeople.

Dewey was a beacon of hope for people going through some tough times. He seemed to believe that everything would turn out okay, and he made others believe it, too. For that and many other reasons, he will always be remembered as a hero.

1987–2006
SPENCER, IOWA

PUSS IN BOOKS

If a library cat like **DEWEY** could talk, he'd probably recommend all kinds of stories about amazing cats. How many of these famous kitty characters do you know?

THE CAT IN THE HAT
The zany kitty in the striped hat made this Dr. Seuss classic one of the top kids' books of all time.

THE CHESHIRE CAT
The riddle-speaking cat with a lingering grin in Lewis Carroll's *Alice's Adventures in Wonderland* has been a feline fan favorite since 1865.

CROOKSHANKS
Hermione's magical pet in the Harry Potter books by J.K. Rowling is half-cat and half-Kneazle, and has an uncanny ability to detect anyone who is untrustworthy or devious.

LORD CAT
The powerful lord in Ed Young's *The Cat from Hunger Mountain* learns a difficult lesson about what really matters to live a happy life.

MRS. TABITHA TWITCHIT
Beatrix Potter's delightfully named shopkeeper is a mother to three unruly kittens—Moppet, Mittens, and Tom Kitten.

PETE

This blue cat who always keeps his cool is the star of this series by James Dean and Eric Litwin, which now includes even more animal friends, from alligators to squirrels.

PUSS IN BOOTS

This clever fairy-tale cat uses his feline wits to win his penniless master a fortune and a princess's hand in marriage.

RUM TUM TUGGER, MACAVITY, SKIMBLESHANKS, AND OTHERS

The whimsically named felines in T. S. Eliot's collection of poems, *Old Possum's Book of Practical Cats,* first appeared in letters written to the author's godchildren.

SKIPPYJON JONES

Judy Schachner's series follows this Siamese cat who believes he's a dog as he adventures everywhere from the circus to a fairy-tale forest with his furry friends.

SNOWBELL

The cat in E. B. White's *Stuart Little* dreams of having the family's mouse-son for a snack and can't be trusted for a moment.

TAO

The Siamese cat in *The Incredible Journey* by Sheila Burnford travels 300 miles through the Canadian wilderness with two canine friends to find their masters.

DOORKINS
THE CATHEDRAL KITTY WHO MET A QUEEN

When a stray tabby showed up at the door of London's Southwark Cathedral, her timing couldn't have been better. The cathedral needed a mouser and Doorkins Magnificat (as she was named) seemed heaven-sent.

Over the years, Doorkins has come to know the secret nooks and crannies of the ancient cathedral better than anyone else. Churchgoers can spy her snoozing in the choir stalls, napping in the churchyard, or burrowing into the hay of the Nativity manger during Christmas services. She even has her very own gargoyle, a stone carving of her face gazing down upon her admirers.

Doorkins enjoys church music and listening to sermons, although she sometimes wanders off before they are finished. She also enjoys weddings. She once took everyone by surprise when she escorted a bride down the aisle, much to the delight of the guests.

Doorkins is very popular with visitors, many of whom come just to meet her. But her most famous visitor by far was the queen of England, Elizabeth II.

When Her Majesty came to see the cathedral's new stained-glass window, Doorkins was asleep on a big chair directly below it. The queen came to a halt the moment she spotted the dozing kitty. Perhaps she was remembering the old nursery rhyme, "Pussycat, pussycat, where have you been? I've been to London to visit the Queen."

The queen asked, "Does this cat live here?" She seemed quite impressed to learn that the answer was yes. Doorkins slept through this entire exchange, clearly unfazed by being in the presence of royalty. She is, after all, a cat.

BORN 2008
ENGLAND

MYSTICAL FELINES

No wonder **DOORKINS** feels at home in a place of worship—cats were once treated like gods **(AND THEY'VE NEVER FORGOTTEN IT)**. In cultures around the world, the mysterious nature of cats has inspired **MYTHS** and **LEGENDS**, **RESPECT** and **FEAR**.

Cats have their own patron saint, **SAINT GERTRUDE OF NIVELLES**. She is also, logically enough, the patron saint for protection from mice and rats.

Nuns at the **MONASTERY OF SAINT NICOLAS OF THE CATS** in Cyprus look after the stray cats that reside there. It's a tradition that spans many centuries!

One time when the **PROPHET MUHAMMAD** was called to prayer, his cat **MUEZZA** was sleeping on the sleeve of his robe. Rather than disturb the cat, he cut off the sleeve.

There is no cat in the Chinese zodiac. However, there is one in the Vietnamese zodiac. If you were born in the **YEAR OF THE CAT** (1963, 1975, 1987, 1999, 2011) then you might be creative and kind, but also stubborn and secretive.

It's often said that cats aren't mentioned in the **BIBLE**, but that's not entirely true. While you won't find so much as the word *CAT* in the Protestant Bible, there is one solitary mention in the Catholic and Orthodox Bibles.

When a new Thai king is crowned, it's an old **BUDDHIST CUSTOM** to give him a **SIAMESE CAT**. The spirit of the old king is said to watch the coronation through the cat's eyes.

The **JEWISH TALMUD** talks about the fine qualities of cats and says that people can learn a great deal from them.

Some **ANCIENT CELTS** believed that cats were a spiritual link between humans and the universe.

Cats were sacred to the **NORSE GODDESS FREYA**, who rode around in a chariot pulled by two large gray cats. Farmers put out saucers of milk for stray cats to win her favor.

In **ROMAN MYTHOLOGY**, the goddess Diana could transform herself into a cat. A handy way to make a quick escape!

CAT FACT

Ever wonder why most **TABBY CATS** have an *M* in the fur on their foreheads? One legend says the newborn Jesus shivered with cold until a tabby cat snuggled next to him in the manger. The **VIRGIN MARY** rewarded the kitty by marking his head with the first letter of her name.

Another story suggests the **PROPHET MUHAMMAD** bestowed this mark after a **TABBY CAT** saved his life by slaying a snake that had slithered up his sleeve.

FAITH
THE CHURCH CAT WHO INSPIRED A NATION

At a humble church in the heart of London, a gray-and-white tabby named Faith kept mice under control and purred at the feet of Father Henry Ross. But this sweet kitty was no ordinary cat.

Soon after Faith gave birth to a kitten named Panda, she started acting a bit odd. She meowed and meowed until the cellar door was opened, then carried Panda down the stairs. Father Ross brought them back up to the warm and cozy rectory. Faith insisted on the cellar. Back and forth it went until Faith finally got her way.

Days later, the rector was away when German planes dropped bombs on the city. It was part of a terrible World War II attack known as the Blitz. Hundreds of people died and many homes and buildings were destroyed.

Father Ross rushed back to London and found his church in ruins. He was told the cats couldn't possibly have survived, but he refused to believe it. He dug through the rubble until he heard a faint meow.

It was Faith! She was filthy but alive, shielding Panda with her body. She was rescued just in time, as moments later the church's roof caved in.

Faith must have been terrified during that long night of bombing, yet she never abandoned her tiny kitten. Newspapers around the world printed her inspiring survival story. Faith became a symbol of strength and courage for the British people.

Faith was awarded a special medal, and the church hung a plaque in honor of the kitty, naming her "The Bravest Cat in the World."

1936–1948
ENGLAND

38

DO CATS HAVE A SIXTH SENSE?

Was it just a coincidence that **FAITH** moved **PANDA** to the safest spot in the church? Or did her powerful feline senses actually warn her of the bombings? While there is little scientific evidence to support the idea that cats have a **SPOOKY** sixth sense, anyone who has ever lived with a cat knows they perceive things in a different way than humans.

HONORÉ DE BALZAC'S cat would meet him on his way home from work each day. On days when the French novelist changed his plans and didn't come home, his cat wouldn't leave the house.

TOMBA often accompanied climbers in the **SWISS ALPS**. One time, he suddenly refused to take another step forward. He ran behind a rock and the climbers followed him. Moments later, an **AVALANCHE** thundered across the path where they'd been standing.

A **PERSIAN CAT'S** owner went away on a long vacation. About a month later, his cat-sitter noticed that he seemed very depressed and refused to eat. Just then, the sitter got a call and learned that the cat's owner had died.

In 2011, many cat owners in **JAPAN** noticed their pets were behaving strangely or seemed stressed out. Days later, there was a terrible **EARTHQUAKE** and **TSUNAMI** that killed thousands of people. Experts believe the cats sensed the disaster ahead of time.

EMMY was a cat who lived on the RMS *Empress of Ireland*. She never missed a trip until one fateful day in 1914 when she refused to come aboard. The following morning, the *Empress* **COLLIDED** with another ship and a thousand passengers were killed.

IS YOUR CAT PSYCHIC?

Here are some signs that suggest a cat might be having a psychic experience:

- 🐾 THE CAT APPEARS TO SEE SOMEONE OR SOMETHING THAT ISN'T ACTUALLY THERE OR IS INVISIBLE TO YOU.

- 🐾 THE CAT AVOIDS CERTAIN ROOMS OR AREAS OF THE HOME OR YARD, OR DISPLAYS FEAR, PROTECTIVENESS, OR EVEN AGGRESSIVENESS IF FORCED TO ENTER THESE AREAS.

- 🐾 THE CAT MEOWS IN A FAMILIAR WAY AT THIN AIR WHEN (SEEMINGLY) NO ONE IS THERE.

NINE LIVES: CAT SURVIVAL STORIES

Cats are born **SURVIVORS**. No wonder people say they have nine lives! Here are nine that beat the odds:

After **BART** was hit by a car in Florida, his owner sadly had him buried. He was shocked to see Bart in the yard **FIVE DAYS LATER**, caked with dirt. In true zombie style, the cat had dug himself out of his own grave.

JACK escaped from his carrier at a New York City airport and was missing for **TWO MONTHS** before he came down through one of the airport's ceiling tiles.

A stray cat was trapped in a Mercedes that was shipped to Australia. **FIFTY DAYS LATER**, the car's new owner found the stowaway. She adopted her and named her **MERCEDES**.

A woman in Alabama drove to work one day, not knowing her cat **RONALD** was clinging for dear life to the car's **ROOFTOP CARGO RACK!**

A cat in New York City survived a **26-FLOOR FALL** from the balcony of her owner's apartment. The terrifying freefall was photographed by window washers. The feline's name? **LUCKY**.

Eighty days after a major earthquake, a **TAIWANESE CAT** was found alive in the rubble of a collapsed building. The cat had lost half her weight but made a full recovery.

FROSTY was found **HALF FROZEN** in a barn. She was so cold that her limbs wouldn't move and her eyes were stuck open. She lived but now wears little sweaters to keep warm.

While her owners were away, **CHLOE** escaped her cat-sitter and got stuck in a **CHIMNEY**. Her owners found her when they returned. She'd gone six weeks without food or water!

PHOENIX crawled inside a parked car to escape the Arizona heat. The car owners drove **400 MILES** before they found her. She'd ridden the whole way inside the bumper!

FÉLICETTE
OUT-OF-THIS-WORLD ASTRO-CAT

Can you imagine sending a cat into space? It sounds crazy but it actually happened.

Back in the 1960s, many countries wanted to be the first to send humans into space. Scientists did lots of tests with dogs and monkeys to get ready. If animals could live in outer space, maybe humans could, too. That was the thinking, anyway.

The Space Race was mainly between the United States and the Soviet Union, yet other countries took part, too. France was the only country with fourteen felines in space training. One was a black-and-white street cat from Paris named Félicette.

After months of training, Félicette was chosen for a voyage into space. She was strapped inside a capsule on a rocket booster and launched nearly 100 miles into the sky. Fifteen minutes later, her capsule floated back to Earth. Everyone cheered when she came out, safe and sound. She was the world's first astro-cat!

Scientists were eager to see if Félicette's brain had changed in any way during her history-making voyage, which included five minutes of fur-raising weightlessness. They learned a great deal, but once humans walked on the Moon, her story was largely forgotten. Even worse, for many years, a male cat named Felix mistakenly got all the credit.

There's no longer much reason to send cats, dogs, and primates into space, and many believe it is unethical to do so. Being launched into space isn't exactly a pleasant experience, and unlike human astronauts, animals have no say in the matter. That's why it's so important to remember and honor Félicette for all that she sacrificed in the name of science.

C. 1963–1964
FRANCE

HUMPHREY
CHIEF MOUSER OF THE BRITISH ISLES

Number 10 Downing Street in London is one of the most famous addresses in the world. The British prime minister lives and works there, and so have a number of cats over the years. One of the best-known Number 10 cats was Humphrey.

Humphrey's official role was Chief Mouser to the Cabinet Office of the United Kingdom of Great Britain and Northern Ireland. That just might be the longest job title for a cat ever! There are lots of mice in old buildings like Number 10, so he had plenty of work to do.

Humphrey was unfazed by photographers and ignored world leaders. Even royalty made him yawn. He once had to be shooed out of the path of a visiting king! Another time, he was nearly squashed under the wheels of a car carrying the president of the United States.

The chief mouser made headlines when he was blamed for slaying four baby birds in the garden of Number 10. The prime minister came to his defense and assured the nation that Humphrey was not a serial killer.

Humphrey gained even greater fame after he went missing for three months and everyone assumed the worst. It turned out that he had simply wandered off and been taken in by the staff of the nearby Royal Army Medical College. After reading his obituary in the newspaper, they realized their adopted kitty was no ordinary stray. He was swiftly returned and everyone doted on him. As well they should.

A former stray, Humphrey spent eight years serving three prime ministers and became one of the most admired cats in all of Great Britain.

1988–2006
ENGLAND

MIGHTY MOUSERS!

Cats like **HUMPHREY** were the world's first pest-control experts. There have been furry exterminators for the past 10,000 years!

WHAT MAKES A GOOD MOUSER?

Even the most pampered house cat never loses the instinct to hunt. But that doesn't mean all cats are born mousers. Some are too lazy and others just aren't interested. The best mousers are often street-smart shelter cats. One thing's for sure though, keeping a cat hungry doesn't get them going after more mice—top mousers hunt for the thrill of the chase, not for the food.

CATS ON PATROL

Did you know that some homeless cats are recruited to become professional mousers? They go to work at wineries, farms, and other places that don't want to use harsh chemicals to stay mice-free. When it comes to rodents, nothing beats a cat. Just having one around can be enough to make mice freak out and go elsewhere.

SOME OF THE MOST WELL-KNOWN CATS IN THE WORLD HAVE BEEN AMAZING MOUSERS. TAKE A LOOK AT SOME MORE ON THE NEXT PAGE!

CAT FACT

Weirdly enough, there was a time when dead cats were sealed up inside the walls of homes and other buildings to bring good luck and scare away rats!

MOUSER HALL OF FAME

LENINGRAD CATS
When the Nazis put Leningrad under siege in World War II, rats became a huge problem. The city's residents would starve if rodents gobbled up their food supplies. The Red Army rounded up **5,000 CATS** and let them loose to do what they do best. End of problem!

DISNEYLAND CATS
About 200 cats at the famous California theme park head out each night to hunt down little **MICKEYS AND MINNIES**. It's worked like a charm since the 1950s.

VENICE CATS
Venice is an Italian city where the locals' **LOVE OF FELINES** dates back centuries. Cats are sometimes credited for helping save the city from the Black Death in 1348, as they kept the rats that supposedly carried the disease at bay.

BRITISH MUSEUM CATS
Back in the 1950s, there was a colony of **STRAY CATS** at the British Museum in London. The museum kitties kept vermin under control and became famous around the world after they were featured in newspaper articles.

POST OFFICE CATS
Cats were employed as mousers for the British Post Office from 1868 to 1984. One of the most famous was **TIBS THE GREAT**, the Post Office headquarters' top mouse-hunter in the 1950s and early '60s. The stocky tabby kept the building free of mice for fourteen years, and his obituary was printed in the official Post Office magazine.

TURN TO PAGE 120 TO LEARN ABOUT TOWSER, THE GREATEST MOUSER OF THEM ALL!

MATILDA
GUEST DIRECT-FUR AT THE ALGONQUIN

Ever since the 1920s, there's been a kitty on hand to greet guests at New York City's Algonquin Hotel. All their names have been either Hamlet or Matilda. The most famous was Matilda III.

Matilda kept an eye on everything and didn't miss a day of work in seven years. She had her own business cards and an assistant to oversee her social media, naps, and busy schedule.

This glamour-puss made TV appearances, had regular grooming sessions, met her fans, and posed for selfies. Whenever she'd had enough, she would turn and face the wall. She was a bit of a diva, that cat.

She feasted like a queen, dining on crab cakes made by the hotel chef. Her favorite treat was bonito, paper-thin slices of dried fish. One hotel guest would bring her them from Japan whenever he was in town. Matilda knew him on sight and would wait by the elevator until he came down from his room.

Each year on her birthday, Matilda hosted a big fundraising event for New York's animal shelters. The highlight of the event was a cat-themed fashion show. She loved to strut down the catwalk!

Matilda's fans loved to send her gifts, all of which she donated to local shelters. She also received marriage proposals from people eager to wed their cats to her, but she politely declined every last one.

Matilda was a cat adored across the globe, receiving letters and emails from fans as far away as Russia and Australia. She answered each one (with some help), always signing off with the words *Have a* purr-*fect day.*

2006–2017
NEW YORK, NY

MORRIS
AMERICA'S FIRST TV CAT-LEBRITY

No advertising spokes-cat has ever surpassed the success of Morris the Cat. He was the star of TV commercials that made him the most recognized cat in America.

The orange tabby's rags-to-riches story began in Chicago as a shelter cat named Lucky. An animal trainer adopted him for five dollars and had him audition for a cat-food commercial. He had so much charisma that the art director called him "the Clark Gable of cats." No wonder he got the job! He also got a new name: Morris the Cat.

Morris shot his first TV commercial for a popular cat-food company, and the "World's Most Finicky Cat" was a major hit. People loved his hilarious been-there-done-that cat-titude. He was treated like a star and had his own secretary and private chauffeur. Talk shows invited him on as a guest and he "wrote" three books about cat care. But Morris didn't let fame go to his photogenic furry head. He generously made personal appearances on behalf of National Adopt-A-Cat Month and other worthy animal causes.

Morris was honored twice as the Performing Animal Television Star of the Year. The PATSY Award was the animal version of the Oscars. He later went from the small screen to the big screen when he starred in a movie with Hollywood superstar Burt Reynolds.

At the peak of his fame, Morris's face was on cat-food cans everywhere, and he had veto power over any flavor he didn't like. He even visited the president at the White House, where he cosigned the Animal Welfare Act with his paw!

1968–1978
HOLLYWOOD, CA

FELINE ENTRE*PURR*-NEURS

MORRIS was a trailblazer for future feline stars, including several other rescue cats that have also played the **"WORLD'S MOST FINICKY CAT"** role over the years. Many of these business-savvy pussycats have developed their very own money-making **BRANDS**. *Cat*-ching!

GRUMPY CAT is a kitty who always seems to be **FROWNING**. Originally named Tardar Sauce (yes, that's *tardar* not *tartar*), she shot to stardom after her photo was posted online. She's now a spokes-cat for a cat-food company, has "written" several bestsellers, and has raked in millions of dollars so far.

FROST is an Australian cat with over **100,000 FOLLOWERS** on Instagram. Sassy and outspoken, this rescue kitty has a publicist and her own line of merchandise featuring her adorable face.

MARU is the most popular cat on **YOUTUBE**, with more than 210 million views (and counting). His name means "round" in Japanese, and his chubby physique has won the Scottish Fold legions of fans around the world. In addition to his videos, Maru earns his kibble from advertisements and sales of DVDs and books.

LIL BUB is an internet star simply because she's so **CUTE**. She was born with several genetic mutations, one of which makes her tongue stick out on a permanent basis. Much of the money Lil Bub earns from appearances goes to charity. She also gives back by appearing in advertisements for animal welfare groups free of charge.

COLONEL MEOW earned a **GUINNESS WORLD RECORD** for having the longest cat fur ever recorded, at a whopping 9 inches! His unusual appearance has endeared him to legions of fans on social media.

COOPER lives in Seattle and wears a lightweight **DIGITAL CAMERA** on his collar once a week, which snaps a new photo from a cat's unique perspective every two minutes. Some of his images of the sky, grass, and leaves are beautifully abstract; others are whimsical and playful, like his shot of plastic pink flamingos in someone's backyard.

DID YOU KNOW?
CATS IS ONE OF THE MOST SEARCHED WORDS ON THE INTERNET. #CAT HAS BEEN USED AS AN INSTAGRAM HASHTAG OVER 100 MILLION TIMES, AND CAT VIDEOS ON YOUTUBE HAVE BEEN VIEWED BY BILLIONS OF PEOPLE!

MOURKA
GRAVITY-DEFYING BALLET STAR

Famous choreographer George Balanchine worked with many talented ballet dancers over the years, but his favorite was a former alley cat named Mourka.

Cats are naturally graceful and flexible, and Mourka easily learned various ballet moves. He spent hours with Mr. B (as George was known) practicing leaps, turns, and spins in the air. Mr. B joked that he had finally found a body worth choreographing for.

When he wasn't dancing, Mourka enjoyed summers in the country, where he napped in the sun and chased bugs and butterflies. Living in the peace and quiet of the countryside, Mourka developed a taste for some rather odd foods for a cat. He loved asparagus, peas, and potatoes with sour cream! The rest of the year he stayed in a stylish New York City apartment with Mr. B and his former-ballerina wife.

At one of Balanchine's Christmas parties, a well-known composer asked to see some of Mourka's trademark moves. Guests later said it was the only time they had ever seen Mr. B nervous before a performance! He wanted everyone to love and admire Mourka as much as he did. And rightly so.

After a popular magazine printed a photo of Mourka doing a spectacular spread-eagled leap, everyone raved about Balanchine's cat. A book deal was soon in the works. *Mourka: The Autobiography of a Cat*, "narrated" by Mourka, had a number of charming photos, including some that made it look like he was dancing alongside real ballerinas. The 1964 book made Mourka one of the first pre-internet cat celebrities.

C. 1960–UNKNOWN
NEW YORK, NY

GO, PUSSYCAT, GO!

Most cats will never become a feline ballet star like **MOURKA**. Yet all cats have a natural athletic ability that rivals even the greatest human Olympians. They are **CAT-THLETES**, with bodies designed to escape danger and hunt prey.

All too often, indoor cats don't get enough exercise to satisfy their natural hunting instincts and keep fit and trim. Exercise not only burns calories, improves muscle tone, and reduces a cat's appetite, it also keeps a cat **MENTALLY STIMULATED**.

Some cats are very active by nature. Others may need some motivation in the form of treats or toys. Here are a few ideas to get your cat moving:

- TOYS THAT ENCOURAGE CHASING AND POUNCING ARE GREAT FOR CATS. SOME SIMPLE OPTIONS ARE CRUMPLED-UP PIECES OF PAPER, CATNIP-FILLED TOYS, SPRINGS, AND WALL- OR DOOR-MOUNTED TOYS.

- CAT TREES AND ELEVATED PERCHES CAN HELP SATIATE YOUR CAT'S DESIRE TO CLIMB. CATS LOVE TO GET UP HIGH, WHERE THEY CAN SAFELY OBSERVE EVERYTHING GOING ON AROUND THEM.

- FORAGING TOYS (ALSO CALLED FOOD PUZZLES, PUZZLE FEEDERS AND TREAT DISPENSERS) HELP SATISFY A CAT'S NATURAL INSTINCT TO SEARCH FOR FOOD.

- INTERACTIVE TOYS, SUCH AS WAND TOYS WITH STRINGS, FEATHERS, AND FABRIC STRIPS ATTACHED, ARE A FUN WAY TO GET KITTY MOVING. PLAYING WITH YOUR CAT IS ALSO A BONDING EXPERIENCE!

- SOME CATS ENJOY LASER POINTERS, WHICH HAVE A PINPOINT OF LIGHT THAT CAN BE CHASED AROUND ON THE FLOOR. NOW AND THEN, BE SURE TO GIVE YOUR CAT A CHANCE TO "CATCH" SOMETHING BY POINTING THE LASER AT A TOY.

- TRAIN YOUR CAT TO PERFORM TRICKS USING YUMMY TREATS. FOR EXAMPLE, YOU CAN TEACH YOUR CAT TO RUN TO YOU FROM ACROSS THE ROOM WHEN YOU SHAKE A BOX OF TREATS.

- GIVE YOUR CAT SOME SAFE TIME OUTDOORS BY BUILDING AN OUTDOOR ENCLOSURE (SOMETIMES CALLED A "CATIO").

CAT TIP

Choose cat toys thoughtfully, avoiding anything with string or small pieces that your cat may try to swallow. It's also a good idea to rotate toys, putting some out of sight, then reintroducing them later. This keeps the toys "fresh" so that kitty doesn't get bored playing with the same toys over and over.

CAT-THLETE HALL OF FAME

DIDGA lives in Australia and is the world's most athletic cat. She holds the Guinness World Record for doing twenty tricks—the "most tricks performed by a cat in one minute." She can ride a skateboard, stop on a coin, jump up into her trainer's hands, and roll over and play dead. That's just for starters!

TURN THE PAGE FOR A CLOSER LOOK AT A CAT'S *PURR*-FECTLY DESIGNED ANATOMY.

THE CAT FROM NOSE TO TAIL

- CATS HAVE A UNIQUE PATTERN ON THEIR **NOSE**, MUCH LIKE A HUMAN FINGERPRINT.

- CAT **JAWS** ONLY MOVE UP AND DOWN. THEY TEAR AND CRUSH THEIR FOOD RATHER THAN CHEW IT.

- CATS USE THEIR BARBED, SANDPAPER-LIKE **TONGUE** TO GROOM THEMSELVES AND LAP UP WATER.

- A CAT PURRS BY VIBRATING THE **VOICE BOX** IN ITS THROAT.

- CATS USE THEIR **WHISKERS** TO DECIDE IF THEY CAN FIT THROUGH A SMALL SPACE.

- CATS HAVE GREAT NIGHT **VISION** BUT CAN'T SEE IN TOTAL DARKNESS.

- EACH CAT **EAR** HAS THIRTY-TWO MUSCLES AND CAN ROTATE 180 DEGREES.

- CATS HAVE AMAZING **HEARING**, ESPECIALLY HIGH-PITCHED SOUNDS HUMANS CAN'T DETECT.

- CATS HAVE MORE NERVE CELLS IN THE VISUAL AREAS OF THEIR **BRAIN** THAN HUMANS AND MOST OTHER MAMMALS.

- THE **COLLARBONE** ISN'T CONNECTED TO OTHER BONES SO CATS CAN SQUEEZE INTO TIGHT SPOTS.

- ALL KITTENS ARE BORN WITH BLUE **EYES**.

- CATS HAVE A **STOMACH** DESIGNED TO DIGEST RAW MEAT (NOT PLANTS!).

- CATS' **LIMBS** ARE SUPER MUSCULAR.

- FEMALE CATS TEND TO BE **RIGHT-PAWED**, AND MALE CATS TEND TO BE **LEFT-PAWED**.

- CATS SWEAT THROUGH THEIR **PAWS**.

- **GLANDS** AROUND THE FACE, TAIL, AND FRONT PAWS PRODUCE A SCENT UNIQUE TO EACH CAT.

- CATS HAVE A DOUBLE LAYER OF **FUR** THAT KEEPS THEM FROM GETTING TOO COLD OR WET.

- THE POSITION OF A CAT'S **TAIL** CAN REVEAL WHAT THEY'RE THINKING.

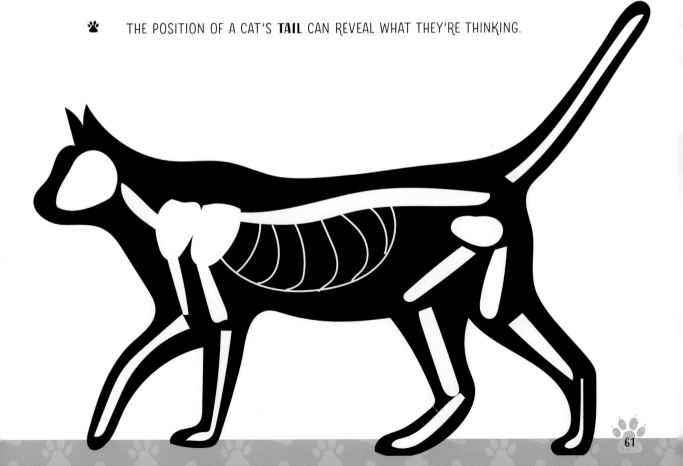

MRS. CHIPPY
EXPLORER CAT ABOARD THE *ENDURANCE*

Mrs. Chippy traveled to the Antarctic aboard Ernest Shackleton's infamous ship, *Endurance*. He belonged to Harry "Chippy" McNish, the ship's carpenter. The crew joked that Chippy's cat followed him around like a housewife, so that's how he got his name. Even though he was actually a male cat!

Mrs. Chippy could climb the rigging and tiptoe along the ship's narrow rails in even the roughest weather. He wasn't a fan of the sled dogs kept on board but grew bold enough to saunter across their kennels, which drove the dogs nuts.

Not long into the voyage, the ship got stuck in ice. And it stayed stuck for nine months! Things got worse when the ship began to break apart from the ice's pressure. Mrs. Chippy napped throughout much of this ordeal, a feat the men found rather comforting. Their situation didn't seem quite so grim with a cat purring away.

Captain Ernest Shackleton finally decided to abandon ship and head for the nearest land, several hundred miles away. To have any chance of survival, they were told they could only take what was absolutely essential. This meant no Mrs. Chippy.

This news was a terrible blow for McNish and the rest of the crew. Their furry friend had been a fine companion during some very tough times. When the fateful day came, each man sadly said goodbye to Mrs. Chippy. A bowl of sardines was prepared, his favorite treat. He slurped them down, then curled up for a nap from which he would never awaken.

Many years later, Mrs. Chippy was symbolically reunited with his beloved master when a life-size bronze statue of the cat was placed atop McNish's grave in New Zealand.

UNKNOWN–1915
SCOTLAND

CATS ON THE MOVE

MRS. CHIPPY wasn't the only cat to travel long distances. There are many others that went a dizzying number of miles, either by chance or by choice. Here are just a few:

When a family in Australia moved to a new house, they took their cat **JESSIE** but left her brother behind. Jessie disappeared soon after the big move. Fifteen months later, she turned up **2,000 MILES AWAY** at the family's old house, where she and her brother were reunited.

In 1919, **WHOOPSIE** was the first cat to **CROSS THE ATLANTIC** from Britain to America by air. He and his human sidekick were stowaways on board an airship.

A cat named **WILLOW** turned up at a New York City shelter. Luckily, she had a microchip and was soon reunited with her family. No one has yet figured out how she got from her home in Colorado to New York, a distance of some **1,800 MILES**.

EMILY found her way inside a shipping container that was sent from Wisconsin to a factory in France. The workers tracked down her owners and an airline flew her home in style—**IN BUSINESS CLASS!**

HAMLET escaped from his carrier inside the cargo hold of a Canadian plane. He was found behind a panel seven weeks later, after traveling about **360,000 MILES**. He now holds the Guinness World Record for "most traveled cat"!

DID YOU KNOW?
CATS HAVE AN INCREDIBLE ABILITY TO FIND THEIR WAY HOME. HOW DO THEY DO IT? SCIENTISTS AREN'T SURE, BUT ONE THEORY IS THAT THEY NAVIGATE USING THE EARTH'S MAGNETIC FIELD.

One-eyed cat **GINGER** escaped from his vet during one of the worst winters in British history. It took **TEN DAYS**, but he made it home, battling deep snow and blizzards and thirty major road crossings to get there.

NORA
CATCERTO KITTY

Nora was adopted by a piano teacher and grew up in a house filled with music. She spent lots of time in the music room, cat-napping in students' book bags and sitting under the piano. When no one was playing the instrument, Nora would chase her reflection on the piano's shiny lid.

When she was about a year old, Nora decided to try playing the piano herself. She hopped on the stool and gently put one paw, then the other, on the keys. She must have thought it made a lovely sound, as she started practicing nearly every day.

Nora was such a natural, she even played duets with the students! One day, someone made a video of her and posted it online. The video, *Practice Makes Purr-fect*, went viral.

Other videos soon followed, and now she has millions of fans across the globe. Even fellow musician Billy Joel is an admirer and once sent her a nice card. Nora has her own Facebook page and website, where fans can stock up on Nora-branded merchandise (like calendars, DVDs, and a "Nora for President" T-shirt).

But Nora is much more than just an internet celebrity. She's a genuine concert pianist. In fact, a composer named Mindaugas Piečaitis created a piece of music called "CATcerto" to showcase her unique talent. The four-minute composition premiered at a grand concert hall in Lithuania. A video of Nora as the "featured soloist" played on a giant screen behind the chamber orchestra throughout the performance.

"CATcerto" now holds a Guinness World Record as the first piano concerto ever composed for a cat. *Brava!*

BORN 2004
PHILADELPHIA, PA

LIGHTS, CAMERA, CATNIP!

NORA isn't the only cat who loves to perform. Some cats get jobs as professional actors.

Cats are known for having short attention spans and being **INDEPENDENT** and strong-willed. So how are cats trained to do things on command? The answer is clicker training and **TREATS**.

CLICKERS are small devices that make an easy-to-hear sound. When a cat does something the trainer wants, he hears the clicker and gets a treat. Action, clicker, treat. It takes time and patience but it works!

Sometimes a film requires a certain **BREED**. Other roles might call for a cat that's super friendly and outgoing. Or can sit still for a long time. Or is good at jumping up on stuff. Or doesn't mind being held.

It isn't easy to find all these skills in a single cat. That's why most cats in movies are played by multiple felines. One example of this is the **SIAMESE CAT** in the 1958 film *Bell, Book and Candle*, who was played by twelve different kitties! Why so many? It's hard to teach one cat to do twelve tricks. It's easier to teach twelve cats to do one trick each!

SEE THE NEXT PAGE FOR SOME OF THE BEST FELINE THESPIANS.

MOVIE STAR CATS

DC was one of several Siamese cats who starred alongside Hayley Mills in the 1965 Disney film *That Darn Cat!*, a live-action film about two sisters and their tomcat.

ARTHUR was a pure white spokes-cat for a British brand of cat food for nearly ten years in the mid-1960s and '70s. He was hired for his ability to nimbly dip his paw into a tin of food on command.

MILO starred in *The Adventures of Milo and Otis*, a film about an orange tabby kitten and her canine buddy. All the actors are animals—there are no humans whatsoever in this film, and that alone makes it worth seeing.

Despite his decidedly uncreative name, **ORANGEY** was a ginger tabby who came to fame playing various film and TV roles back in the 1950s. He was most famous for playing Cat, Audrey Hepburn's kitty in *Breakfast at Tiffany's*.

PUMPKIN and **CRACKERJACK** are red Persians who played the role of Hermione Granger's pet, Crookshanks, in the *Harry Potter* films. The feline character Mrs. Norris was played by three Maine Coons—**MAXIMUS**, **ALANIS**, and **CORNELIUS**—each trained to perform a specific action.

The hairless Sphynx in the Austin Powers movies was played by two cats, **TED NUDE-GENT** and **MEL GIBSKIN**.

OSCAR
THE CUDDLY GRIM REAPER

If you ever see Oscar and he curls up in your lap, you have good reason to worry. It's likely you only have a few hours left to live.

Oscar lives at a New England nursing home and has a very rare talent. He knows when people are about to pass away. About two to four hours beforehand, he will hop up onto the bed of a soon-to-die patient and snuggle next to them. His predictions are so accurate that whenever he is found with a patient, the staff calls the family and a priest ASAP.

So far, Oscar has been right about one hundred times. His gift might sound a tad creepy, but it isn't. He is a wonderful source of comfort to those on the brink of the "Great Beyond," calmly purring away at their sides. He helps patients' families, too, bringing a sense of peace and serenity at a very difficult time. Many people are so touched by his gentle compassion that they thank him in their loved ones' obituaries.

The big question is, of course, how does he do it? No one knows for certain. One theory is that Oscar's feline super senses can detect something humans can't, such as ketones, which are chemicals given off by dying cells. Another theory is that Oscar has some kind of psychic connection with dying patients, sensing changes in their behavior before they pass. Perhaps his role here on Earth is to help people cross over to the "other side."

However he does it, Oscar's gifts are so one of a kind that a doctor at the nursing home was inspired to write a book about him called *Making Rounds with Oscar: The Extraordinary Gift of an Ordinary Cat*. For a cat who isn't particularly sociable, he's won many hearts by helping people when they need him most.

BORN 2005
PROVIDENCE, RI

SPOOKY CATS

Is it possible that cats like **OSCAR** can sense the energy of the dead? Next time you see a cat staring at nothing, he might be seeing something you can't—like a **GHOST!**

There are many stories of cats haunting those who mistreated them. **GHOST CATS** can also be kitties that died suddenly and aren't quite ready to leave their owners. Here's some spooky stuff that's fun to think about:

In **SCOTTISH FOLKLORE**, a black cat known as the **CAT SÌTH** was said to be a witch who could turn into a kitty eight times. The ninth time, the witch would stay stuck as a cat!

A black cat called **DEMON CAT** is said to have haunted the basement of the United States Capitol Building in **WASHINGTON, DC**. He has glowing red eyes and appears out of nowhere, scaring the living hairballs out of people. Luckily, he hasn't been sighted since World War II, so perhaps he's moved on.

THE CONGLETON CAT was a white cat that went missing in England in the late 1800s. He finally showed up at his owner's door but refused to come inside. After a few moments, he slowly **VANISHED**, just like the Cheshire Cat in *Alice's Adventures in Wonderland*.

THE CHÂTEAU DE COMBOURG in France is said to be haunted by a former resident with a wooden leg. His ghost is sometimes accompanied by a **BLACK CAT**, possibly the ghost of a kitty found buried inside the walls of the castle.

THE CRESCENT HOTEL in Arkansas has many spirit guests, including a ginger tabby named **MORRIS**. He was the hotel cat many years ago and apparently has never left.

A **BAKENEKO** ("ghost cat") is the name given to a mythological Japanese creature that starts out as a regular cat but transitions into something else. They can walk on their hind legs and grow to human size. They also have the ability to change form, summon fireballs, and use their tails to start fires. Years ago, it was common practice to cut young cats' tails as a preventive measure.

DID YOU KNOW?
A CAT NAMED **ELVIS** AT A SCOTTISH WHISKY DISTILLERY ISN'T A GHOST HIMSELF—HE'S A GHOST HUNTER. HE CAPTURED IMAGES OF A LEGENDARY SPOOK ON A CAT CAM ATTACHED TO HIS COLLAR!

OSCAR
THE BIONIC CAT

It was harvest season on the island of Jersey in the Channel Islands, and a black cat named Oscar was dozing in a field. No one knows quite how it happened, but there was a terrible accident and Oscar's hind paws were cut off.

He was rushed to the local animal hospital and his owners prepared for the worst. Cats can lead a fairly normal life with three paws, but only two? It seemed likely they'd have to put their beloved kitty to sleep.

But there was one tiny glimmer of hope. A vet on the UK mainland had used implants to replace missing limbs on dogs—perhaps he could do the same for Oscar? It was a long shot, as no cat had ever had this surgery before and no animal had ever had two feet replaced, but it was Oscar's only chance.

In a three-hour operation, veterinary surgeon Noel Fitzpatrick inserted thin rods into Oscar's hind leg bones. Each rod poked out at the end so that steel feet could be screwed on later. The surgery went well and Oscar seemed determined to live. He had nerves of steel and legs to match!

After eight months of recovery, Oscar was allowed to go home. He click-clacked his way around as his high-tech feet hit the stone floor. He was so active that he wore out his first steel feet and had to get new ones.

There were other setbacks and surgeries, but Oscar came through it all like a champ. His owner wrote a book about his amazing story and he was featured on TV shows. Oscar not only leads a normal life, but he's an inspiration for other injured pets (and people, too). He also holds a Guinness World Record for being the first animal with two bionic legs.

BORN 2007
JERSEY, CHANNEL ISLANDS

FELINE MUSES

OSCAR the bionic cat inspired a vet to try something that had never been done before. Here are some other kitties that inspired greatness:

Whenever the famous astronomer **EDWIN HUBBLE** worked at his desk, his cat **NICOLAS COPERNICUS** would sprawl across as many pages as he could. Hubble told his wife, "He is helping me."

A black cat named **HODGE** was the loyal companion of **SAMUEL JOHNSON**, famous for compiling his *Dictionary of the English Language* (1755). A statue of Hodge in London is inscribed with words that Dr. Johnson once used to describe him: "A very fine cat indeed."

Author **MARK TWAIN** (Samuel Clemens) liked cats more than people. He had as many as nineteen at a time, all with wacky names such as **BEELZEBUB, BUFFALO BILL,** and **ZOROASTER**.

EDWARD LEAR, who wrote "The Owl and the Pussy-Cat," doted on his cat **FOSS**. When the poet built a new house, he made it just like the old one so Foss could easily find his way around.

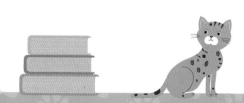

PIERRE-AUGUSTE RENOIR'S cats were featured in many of his paintings. The artist often warmed his stiff fingers on the kitties lounging in his studio. That's actually one way to prove a Renoir painting is the real thing—check for strands of cat hair caught in the paint!

NIKOLA TESLA had a black cat named **MAČAK** when he was a boy. One time, his hand produced a shower of static electricity as he stroked the kitty's fur. It sparked the inventor's obsession with electricity.

SIR ISAAC NEWTON'S experiments were often interrupted by his cat scratching at the door, so he supposedly had a carpenter cut two holes in it—a large hole for **SPITHEAD** and a smaller one for her kittens. Was this the world's first cat flap? Or is the story just a story? No one knows for sure.

SALVADOR DALÍ was an eccentric Surrealist painter from Spain who lived during the twentieth century. His cat, **BABOU**, was just as unique as his owner, so the two were a perfect pair. Babou was an ocelot, a dwarf leopard breed native to Central and South America.

ANDY WARHOL was an artist who was famous for his screen prints of stars like Marilyn Monroe and Elizabeth Taylor. He also painted hundreds of cans of Campbell's soup, Coca-Cola bottles, and cats. His best friend **SAM** was a Siamese cat who was featured in many of his drawings and paintings.

PITOUTCHI
THE KITTY WHO FOOLED THE GERMAN ARMY

In times of war, cats have served as mousers, mascots, and good luck charms. One cat certainly brought luck to Lieutenant Lekeux of the Belgian Army.

Lekeux found an orphaned kitten that was so tiny he had to be fed with an eyedropper. The lieutenant named him Pitoutchi because that was the sound the cat made whenever he sneezed. Pitoutchi never grew very big but he was devoted to his human. He'd walk next to Lekeux wherever he went. If it was raining, he'd jump up on to Lekeux's shoulder. They were never apart for long.

Lekeux was out on patrol with Pitoutchi on his shoulder when he spotted enemy soldiers. They were digging a new trench, and that was important information. He hid in a shell hole and made a sketch to take back to camp. He was so focused that he didn't see three Germans heading his way until it was too late.

The lieutenant froze and prayed the soldiers hadn't seen him. But one called out in German, "He's in the hole!" Lekeux expected to be captured or killed any second.

Pitoutchi chose this life-or-death moment to suddenly launch himself out of the shell hole. He sprang straight up into the air and landed on a nearby piece of wood. The Germans were so startled that they fired twice, missing the cat both times.

The soldiers laughed at themselves, thinking they had mistaken a cat for the enemy. They moved on and Lekeux scurried back to camp, his sketch in hand. The tiny white cat who had saved his life rode in triumph upon his shoulder.

1914-UNKNOWN
BELGIUM

POLAR BEAR
THE CAT WHO CAME FOR CHRISTMAS

On a snowy Christmas Eve in New York City, a filthy, wet, bone-thin cat shivered in a dark alleyway. He caught the eye of an animal-rights crusader and journalist named Cleveland Amory. Neither knew it then, but both of their lives had just changed forever.

Amory took the scrawny kitty home to his apartment and gave him a bath. The gray cat turned out to be pure white under all that dirt and grime. Polar Bear (as he came to be named) quickly made himself at home and they became best friends.

Amory wrote a book about their first year together called *The Cat Who Came for Christmas*. It told the story of the street cat with a mind of his own and the grumpy guy who had never owned a cat before. The book was an immediate hit, and two bestselling sequels followed. Polar Bear became the most famous cat in America.

But Polar Bear didn't care about being a celebrity. He wasn't interested in TV appearances or doing book tours. He didn't want to meet movie stars or be on the cover of magazines. Those 11,000 fan letters he received? They didn't excite him either, although he did like the ones that contained catnip. As Polar Bear saw it, fame wasn't all it was cracked up to be.

Polar Bear made several visits to Black Beauty Ranch, the refuge Amory opened in Texas for mistreated and abandoned animals. He continued to be an inspiration to a man who helped countless animals, and will always be remembered for putting a face on the special bond cats share with their humans.

1977–1992
NEW YORK, NY

10 WAYS TO HELP CATS IN NEED

CLEVELAND AMORY never had a cat until he met **POLAR BEAR**, but he loved animals from a young age and was dedicated to helping them. No matter what age you are, there are all sorts of ways to help kittens and cats in need.

HERE ARE A FEW IDEAS:

1. Ask people to have their pets **SPAYED** and **NEUTERED**. Sterilization means fewer homeless cats living on the streets or in overcrowded animal shelters.

2. RAISE MONEY for shelter cats by doing odd jobs such as mowing the lawn or babysitting, by organizing a bake sale, or by fundraising for an animal charity.

3. VOLUNTEER at a shelter. From cleaning cages and filling food bowls to socializing young kittens and helping set up a shelter's online presence, there's a lot you can do as a volunteer.

4. ADOPT, don't shop. There are millions of adorable kitties out there waiting for a forever home. Adopt a kitty from a shelter or an animal rescue organization, not from a breeder. Think first before adopting, though, as it's a big responsibility.

5. SET UP A DONATION DRIVE. Collect items shelters need such as cat food, cat litter, toys, old towels, and blankets.

6. ASK FOR DONATIONS, not gifts, on your birthday or for special occasions. Friends and family can donate to an animal shelter or charity in your name. Helping others in need is the best gift of all.

7. FOSTER A CAT. Many kitties need a place to stay while they wait to be adopted. It can be hard to say goodbye sometimes, but it's great to know you've helped a cat on its journey to a new family.

8. SPEAK UP! If you see an animal in trouble, tell someone or go to the authorities.

9. BE KIND TO CATS OF ALL AGES. Kittens tend to get more attention because they are so small and cute and playful. But senior cats are equally wonderful, so make it a point to give older cats some extra love, too.

10. SPREAD THE WORD. Post a photo of a cat that needs a home on social media. It only takes one person to see your message and decide to adopt!

CAT TIP

For more information and other ways to help, see the list of websites on page 145. You'll find links to a number of sites that offer great advice about cat care, inspiring rescue stories, feline facts and stats, cat photos, videos, and much more.

PYRO
THE FLYING CAT OF WORLD WAR II

Pyro was born on a Royal Air Force base in Scotland. He was just a kitten when he tiptoed into the darkroom of photographer Bob Bird, looking for a warm place to stay. Bird adopted the tabby and named him Pyro.

Pyro would hang around the airbase waiting for Bird to return from his top-secret flying missions. He seemed lonely whenever he was left alone, so Bird began carrying him around in his flight jacket. Bird would whistle as he headed out to the airfield and Pyro would come running. This was a cat who loved to fly.

Pyro helped the war effort in his own unique way. Flying at high altitude on a bitterly cold day, Pyro was snuggled as usual inside Bird's jacket. Ice coated the wings of their plane and it crash-landed into the sea! Awaiting rescue, Bird started to get severe frostbite. He used the cat's body heat to warm his hands. Doctors later told Bird that Pyro had saved his fingers.

Pilots on base thought of Pyro as a good luck charm that could chase away gremlins—imaginary creatures that they believed caused accidents. They would ask to borrow the cat whenever they flew dangerous missions. Bird agreed as long as it was okay with Pyro. The cat seemed to know how important it was to keep everyone's spirits up.

As Pyro's closest buddy throughout the war, Bird would have been proud to know that his cat's wartime heroism was honored many years later. The fearless flying kitty received a special award for bravery from the People's Dispensary for Sick Animals.

1942–1945
SCOTLAND

ROOM 8
LEGENDARY SCHOOL MASCOT

When a thin tabby strolled into a sixth-grade classroom in California, the children were delighted. They gave him some milk and shared their lunches with him. He came back the next day and followed them inside. And there he stayed. The school adopted the cat and named him after the room where he spent most of his time.

The students gave Room 8 so many treats that he soon went from scrawny to plump. The school thought it best to appoint one lucky student to be his official cat feeder. This job was the envy of the entire school! At the end of the school year, Room 8 joined the graduating sixth-graders for their class photograph, held in the arms of his feeder.

No one knew much about Room 8's past or where he went during school breaks. So the head teacher did some sleuthing and discovered that their beloved mascot had been badly treated by his former owners. He must have come to the school in search of a new and better life. He definitely found it!

After a newspaper printed his story, Room 8 was invited to attend cat shows and other local events. A magazine did an article about him and the head teacher wrote a book. He was even featured in a TV documentary. He got lots of fan mail—about 10,000 letters in his lifetime! Many were addressed simply to "Room 8, Los Angeles, California," yet they made their way to him.

Room 8 became such a celebrity that his paw prints were embedded in wet cement in front of the school. His legacy lives on, even to this day.

1947–1965
LOS ANGELES, CA

LIFE-SAVING CATS

Cats like **ROOM 8** can be just as loyal as "man's best friend." They are there through thick and thin and look out for the people who look out for them. But some cats go **ABOVE AND BEYOND** to show their owners just how much they care. A number of kitties have even saved their owners' lives, or the lives of others.

Four-year-old Jeremy was on a bike in front of his home when a neighbor's dog attacked him. His family's cat **TARA** went after the dog, scaring it and chasing it away. There's even a YouTube video showing the whole event, which has now gone viral.

When Gary fell from his wheelchair and couldn't reach the phone to call for help, his cat **TOMMY** managed to push the phone's speed-dial button and called the emergency services himself.

Trudy was asleep when **SCHNAUTZIE** jumped on her chest and pawed at her. She got up and found a major gas leak. Her cat had prevented a possible explosion.

Susan was a diabetic who fell unconscious in her bathroom. **CHARLEY** sensed something was wrong. The cat woke up Susan's husband and led him to her, just in time to give her a life-saving glucose injection.

When a terrier named Izzy was attacked by a much bigger dog, Izzy's feline buddy **SAMMY** did everything he could to get the vicious dog's attention. The attacker dropped Izzy and chased after Sammy, who escaped up a tree. He saved Izzy's life.

Wendy had a small breast tumor that had gone unnoticed, but **FIDGE** knew something was amiss. He pawed at her chest so many times that she finally went to her doctor. The cat detected the cancer before it had a chance to spread.

A Californian woman found a deadly rattlesnake in her son's room. The family's cat **LUCY** was crouched by the child, putting her own life at risk to protect him from harm.

SAM
THE UNSINKABLE CAT

A cat crept aboard the German warship *Bismarck* just before it headed off on its first World War II mission. The *Bismarck* sank to the bottom of the sea after a fierce battle and there were only a few survivors. The cat was one of them. He was found floating on a board by the crew of a British ship, the HMS *Cossack*. They named him Oscar.

Oscar seemed happy enough to switch sides in the war and spent the next few months with the Royal Navy in the Mediterranean. But then the *Cossack* was torpedoed by a German U-boat. The cat survived that shipwreck, too.

After two doomed ships, the British Navy decided Oscar deserved a new name: Unsinkable Sam. They also thought he'd be better off on an aircraft carrier like the HMS *Ark Royal*, which was said to be a lucky vessel. Oddly enough, it too was torpedoed just weeks later.

Poor Sam! He was found clinging to a floating plank once again. Plucked from the sea by a passing boat, he was described as "angry but quite unharmed." Three shipwrecks in a single year, no wonder he wasn't too happy.

Well, enough was enough and Sam was transferred to land duty. He became the chief mouser at the home of the governor of Gibraltar. He later retired to a home for sailors in Great Britain, where he happily lived out the rest of his days.

Today at the National Maritime Museum in Greenwich, England, you can see a pastel portrait of Sam calmly perched on a piece of floating wreckage. He is the only cat to have caught mice for the Nazis as well as the Allies in World War II.

1941–1955
GERMANY/ENGLAND

BATTLE CATS!

Cats are often overlooked in the history of military animals, and that's a real shame. There are many **FASCINATING TALES** about felines in times of **WAR**, like these kitties that lived long ago:

In **500 BC**, war was brewing between **EGYPT** and **PERSIA**. The Persian king, Cambyses II, came up with a bizarre strategy. He knew cats were sacred to the Egyptians, so he let hundreds of cats loose onto the battlefield. It worked! The Egyptian soldiers were so **TERRIFIED** of hurting a kitty that thousands surrendered on the spot. Who knew fluffy felines could be such a powerful weapon?

SIXTEENTH-CENTURY GERMAN SCIENTISTS came up with a cruel plan to use cats to spread poisonous gas. The idea was to attach glass jars filled with gas to the cats' collars and send them into enemy territory. The plan backfired when the cats spun around and ran back toward their own troops. **OOPS!** That was the end of that horrible idea.

In **1854**, British and French troops occupied the Russian port town of **SEVASTOPOL**. A cat called **CRIMEAN TOM** led starving troops to food stores that had been hidden by the Russians. The men adopted the cat in gratitude for saving their lives.

President **ABRAHAM LINCOLN** had a soft spot for cats. One day in 1865, during the Civil War, he was visiting Union army headquarters and came upon three orphaned kittens. He held them gently and ordered his men to give them milk and treat them kindly.

President Lincoln's Civil War nemesis, **GENERAL ROBERT E. LEE**, also loved cats. The leader of the Confederate army shared his tent with some of them, partly for pest control and partly for company.

FELINE WAR HEROES

It's a little-known fact that cats served in both **WORLD WARS** and other conflicts. These **WAR CATS** were mascots, mousers, and morale boosters. Their innocent charm and funny antics reminded people of normal life and the comforts of home.

In **WORLD WAR II**, a British cat named **BOMBER** could tell the difference between RAF planes and enemy planes. If he heard German planes coming, he'd scamper for cover and his family was quick to follow.

Superstitious American pilots supposedly flew a black cat named **CAPTAIN MIDNIGHT** over Germany during **WORLD WAR II**. They wanted him to "cross the path" of Nazi leader Adolf Hitler.

A Russian spy cat named **MOURKA** played a big role in a major **WORLD WAR II** battle. Nicknamed the Battlecat of Stalingrad, this amazing cat risked his life carrying leaflets and messages about the location of German troops.

During the **KOREAN WAR**, a United States marine found a kitten he named **MISS HAP**. He had many marriage proposals after a photo of him bottle-feeding the cat appeared in newspapers. Miss Hap became a mascot for the Press and Information Office.

In **2004**, a kitten wandered into United States Army headquarters in Iraq. **HAMMER** hunted mice and also served as a therapy cat for homesick and stressed-out soldiers. The grateful troops made him an honorary member of their unit and brought him back to America.

DID YOU KNOW?
AS MANY AS 500,000 CATS WORKED AS MOUSERS IN THE MUDDY, RAT-INFESTED TRENCHES OF WORLD WAR I.

SCARLETT
COURAGE UNDER FIRE

New York City firefighters rushed to the scene when a fire broke out in an abandoned garage in Brooklyn. One of the firefighters noticed a scrawny calico cat carrying her kittens away from the flames, one by one. The mother cat was badly burned and her eyes were blistered shut. Unable to see, she touched each kitten with her nose to make sure they were all there—one, two, three, four, five. Then she collapsed, too exhausted to go on.

The firefighter rushed the injured kitties to a nearby animal hospital. Scarlett (as she was later named) was in such bad shape that one staff member burst into tears at the sight of her. But Scarlett was a fighter. After three months, the only signs of her terrible ordeal were her poor vision, misshapen eyes, and the damaged tips of her ears.

Scarlett's incredible courage made headlines around the world. Thousands of people offered to give her or her four surviving kittens a forever home. Scarlett's caretakers thought hard about what would be best for the cats.

The names of the kitties' new families were announced at a crowded press conference. The kittens were adopted in pairs. Scarlett was adopted by a woman who had endured a long and painful recovery after a car accident. She knew what Scarlett had been through and wanted to care for a kitty with special needs. *Purr*-fect!

Scarlett made a number of TV appearances, and people wrote books and articles about her. A special award was created in her honor called the Scarlett Award for Animal Heroism, which is given out to heroic animals to this day.

1995–2008
BROOKLYN, NY

WHY ARE CATS SO WEIRD?

Cats can act pretty **STRANGELY** at times (at least from a human's point of view). Can **YOU** explain feline behavior? Take this quiz to find out!

1.   WHY DO CATS LIKE BOXES?
A)   They're a safe hiding place
B)   They're nice and warm
C)   They're small and cozy

2.   WHY DO CATS HATE GETTING WET?
A)   Not all cats do
B)   Cats can't swim
C)   It makes them look silly

3.   WHY DO CATS LIKE HIGH PLACES?
A)   They feel safer there
B)   It's warmer there
C)   Both of the above

4.   WHY DO CATS USE A LITTER BOX?
A)   They like being tidy
B)   It's instinct
C)   It's fun to play in the sand

5. WHAT ARE THE "ZOOMIES"?

A) When a cat runs around for no apparent reason

B) The spirit of a deceased cat

C) Any toy containing catnip

6. WHY DO CATS GO A BIT CRAZY AROUND CATNIP?

A) They don't—that's a myth

B) The smell makes them hyper

C) No one really knows

7. WHY DO CATS GROOM THEMSELVES SO MUCH?

A) They are bored

B) All kinds of reasons

C) It's a nervous habit

8. WHY ARE HOUSE CATS MOST ACTIVE AT DAWN AND DUSK?

A) They prefer low light to bright daylight

B) They are crepuscular

C) They aren't—that's an old wives' tale

TURN TO PAGE 142 TO SEE HOW YOU DID!

SIMON
BRITISH NAVY WAR HERO

Simon came aboard the British warship *Amethyst* as a kitten and quickly became an excellent mouser and mascot. But it wasn't until a voyage up the Yangtze River that Simon proved himself a war hero as well.

On its way to China, the ship was attacked by Chinese soldiers fighting a civil war. The captain and twenty-four crew members were killed. Many others were badly hurt, including Simon. The ship's doctor treated the cat's burns and injuries, though he wasn't expected to live through the night. But Simon did.

Stranded behind enemy lines, life on board was hot, humid, and boring. And there were rats. LOTS of rats. Simon wasn't fully recovered, yet his hunting skills were needed more than ever. He caught at least one rat a day! After he took out the nastiest rat of all, the crew hailed Simon as a hero. They even promoted him to Able Seacat Simon.

Simon also kept up the spirits of injured sailors. He sat on their beds, kneading his paws and purring. The young men eagerly awaited his visits. He was one of the world's first therapy cats.

The siege dragged on for more than three months. There was no rescue in sight and food was running low. The only solution was to make a daring escape. It worked! The long ordeal was finally over.

News spread of the crew's survival and they were all hailed as heroes—Simon, too! The captain nominated him for the PDSA Dickin Medal, awarded to animals for wartime bravery. Simon was the first—and is still the only cat—to receive this honor.

1947–1949
ENGLAND

RECORD-BREAKING CATS

So many animals have shown incredible **BRAVERY** in wartime that a special medal was created to honor them. Since 1943, the **PDSA DICKIN MEDAL** has been awarded to dogs, pigeons, horses, and one solitary cat—Able Seacat **SIMON**.

HERE ARE SOME OTHER CATS THAT MADE HISTORY IN THEIR OWN FABULOUS FELINE WAYS:

A Texas tabby named **DUSTY** holds the record for having the **MOST KITTENS IN A LIFETIME**: 420.

The **LARGEST LITTER** was nineteen kittens, born to a mama cat in Britain.

When British millionaire Ben Rea died in 1988, he left money to three cat charities, his gardener, mechanic, and plumber, and he gave a friend a house. But most of his fortune went to his cat. With $12.5 million to spend on toys and treats, **BLACKIE** was the **WORLD'S WEALTHIEST CAT**.

Feline sweethearts **PHET** and **PLOY** of Thailand had **THE MOST EXPENSIVE CAT WEDDING** ever. It cost about $24,000 and they had 500 guests!

At nearly 7.5 inches (19 centimeters), the **LONGEST WHISKERS** belonged to **MISSI**, a Maine Coon in Finland.

The **LOUDEST PURR** ever recorded was 86.3 decibels, courtesy of **SMOKEY**, a British cat.

The **WORLD'S LONGEST CAT** was **STEWIE**, a Maine Coon that measured 48.5 inches (123 centimeters) long from the tip of his nose to the end of his tail bone.

The **OLDEST CAT EVER** was **CREME PUFF** in Texas. She lived 38 years and 3 days.

MR. PEEBLES had a genetic defect that made him the **WORLD'S SMALLEST LIVING CAT**. He weighed about 3 pounds and stood just over 6 inches (15 centimeters) high.

The **OLDEST FELINE MOTHER** was a British cat, **KITTY**. She had two kittens at age 30.

ZEUS, an Asian leopard/domestic shorthair cat hybrid, is the **WORLD'S MOST EXPENSIVE CAT**. He had an asking price of nearly $130,000 in 2017.

The **LONGEST JUMP** ever recorded by a cat was in 2013. **ALLEY** in Texas jumped a length of 6 feet (1.8 meters).

SNOWBALL
THE CAT WHO SOLVED A MURDER

When a woman was found murdered on Prince Edward Island in Canada, a leather jacket found near the crime scene became a key piece of evidence. It was splattered with blood and two dozen white hairs.

Tests showed the hairs came from a cat. A detective recalled seeing a white cat at the home of one of the suspects—Snowball, the family pet. If the white hairs came from Snowball, it would provide a link to solve the case.

There was just one hitch. DNA testing on humans was still a relatively new science at the time. And DNA testing on animals? No one had ever done it or wanted to try. But the detective kept making calls until he found an expert who would examine the hairs. And guess what? The hairs matched a blood sample from Snowball!

Now the prosecution had to prove that the other cats on the island didn't have the same DNA. The police rounded up twenty stray cats and tested all of them, too. None of their DNA was anything at all like Snowball's. That made the cat the star witness in the case.

The suspect was found guilty of murder and went to prison for a long, long time. The case also made legal history. It was the first time animal DNA had ever been used in a criminal court trial. Newspaper editors went wild as they tried to outdo each other with catty headlines such as *"Purr*-fect Match," "CAT-astrophe for Criminals," and "Fur-ensic Evidence."

These days, forensic science has come a long way, and fur, blood, and urine from animals are often used to help solve crimes. Some countries even have cat and dog DNA databases. Thanks to Snowball, pets can now rat on bad guys without even moving a whisker.

C. 1994–UNKNOWN
CANADA

SOCKS
AMERICA'S "FIRST CAT"

When Chelsea Clinton, the daughter of Arkansas governer Bill Clinton, saw kittens playing in her piano teacher's garden, one of them leaped into her arms. He seemed to say, "You're my human!" And that's how Socks joined the Clinton family and ended up in the White House when Bill Clinton became the president of the United States.

For his own safety, Socks wasn't allowed to roam the White House grounds. He was kept on a long leash on the South Lawn whenever he went outside. But there were lots of squirrels and birds to chase, and he befriended a stray cat named Slippers.

Whenever it was cold or rainy, Socks would hang out in the East Wing or in his three-story cat house. He also liked to nap on a chair in the office of the president's personal secretary, Betty Currie.

Socks wasn't thrilled about being in the public eye, but he had certain duties as the nation's "First Cat." He visited hospitals, orphanages, and nursing homes, purring on the First Lady's lap and posing for photos. He traveled in a fancy basket adorned with the presidential seal. Once in a while, he even got to ride in a limousine. Socks received piles of fan mail, and retired soldiers kindly helped him answer each letter.

After Chelsea headed off to college, President Clinton adopted a puppy named Buddy. Socks and Buddy sadly didn't get along and no one knew what to do. Luckily, Betty Currie had grown very fond of Socks and invited him to live with her. He was happy to return to civilian life and spent the rest of his days at her home in Maryland.

1990–2009
WASHINGTON, DC

PUSSYCATS IN HIGH PLACES

Other kitties throughout history have lived in splendor, too, just like **SOCKS**! Here's a few of the best high-powered felines:

At the **WHITE HOUSE**, President Teddy Roosevelt once escorted some VIPs down a hallway where his cat **SLIPPERS** was napping. Instead of shooing her away, the president carefully led his guests around the dozing feline.

Catherine the Great treated her cats like royalty at the **WINTER PALACE** in Saint Petersburg, Russia. The palace is now part of the Hermitage, an art museum that's also home to about seventy kitties. The famous **HERMITAGE MOUSERS** are all former strays.

King Louis XVI and Marie Antoinette sent six of their kitties across the ocean for safekeeping during the **FRENCH REVOLUTION**. The royals lost their heads, but the cats supposedly made it all the way to the East Coast of America. Could these kitties have bred with the local cats and evolved to become the large fluffy cat we know as the **MAINE COON?** It's not certain, but it's one theory that makes a great story.

King Louis XV of France had a **WHITE PERSIAN OR ANGORA CAT** and lots of other cats, too. They were allowed to wander wherever they wished at the **PALACE OF VERSAILLES**. He even let them walk across the gambling tables set up for royal guests.

The first pet cat in Japan belonged to Emperor Ichijo. She lived at the **IMPERIAL PALACE** in Tokyo and had a very fancy title—**CHIEF LADY-IN-WAITING OF THE INNER PALACE**.

Queen Victoria was crazy about animals. She doted on a cat named **WHITE HEATHER**, a Persian that lived in the lap of luxury at **BUCKINGHAM PALACE** in London.

Some Roman Catholic popes loved cats and kept them as pets at the **VATICAN IN ROME**. Pope Paul II had his own doctor treat his cats whenever they were ill. Pope Paul VI liked to dress his kitty in miniature papal robes.

STUBBS
ALASKAN TOWN MAYOR

The tiny town of Talkeetna, Alaska, never had an official mayor. Not until the manager of the general store found a kitten without a tail in her parking lot. He became so popular with locals that they made him an honorary mayor.

Mayor Stubbs (as he was known) became something of a tourist attraction. People from all over came to see him at his office at the general store. Out-of-towners loved to say, "Hey, where's the mayor?" or "I have an appointment with the mayor!" The townspeople just rolled their eyes. Stubbs received heaps of fan mail, too. Not many politicians can say that.

One time, the furry orange mayor was attacked by a dog and badly injured. A crowd-funding campaign was set up to help pay for his medical bills. People all over the world sent in donations. Stubbs spent nine days in the animal hospital, but soon returned to his mayoral duties.

The dog attack wasn't Stubbs's only brush with death. He once managed to escape from a pack of BB-gun-wielding teenagers. Another time, he slipped and fell into a restaurant's deep fryer. Thankfully, it was switched off at the time! Then there was the time he hitched a ride out of town on the back of a garbage truck . . . He really was a cat with nine lives, and had the stories to prove it.

Stubbs stopped at a local eatery each afternoon for some catnip-infused water. He liked to sip it from a wineglass. He also wasn't above taking "bribes" (scraps of salmon or crab). But no one seemed to mind. As one town resident put it, "He hasn't voted for anything I wouldn't have voted for."

1997–2017
TALKEETNA, ALASKA

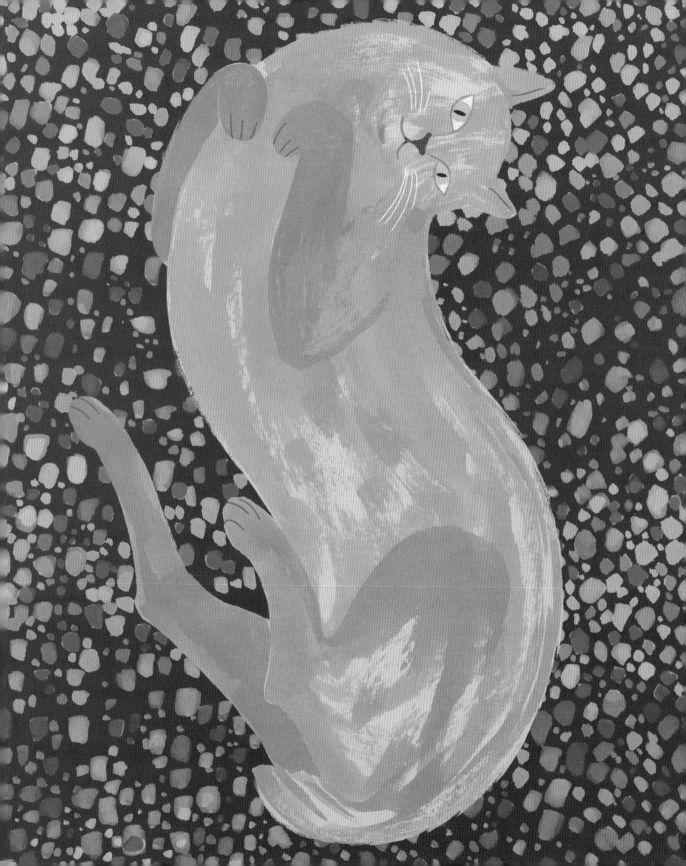

CATS IN CHARGE!

Cats already know they rule the world. But some of them, like **STUBBS**, want to be even bigger **CAT-ALYSTS FOR CHANGE**. Here are seven that ran for political office:

BARSIK won nearly 92 percent of the vote in an unofficial poll for mayor of a Siberian town. Residents were fed up and wanted a different kind of leader. Who better than a cat?

CATMANDO served as co-leader of **BRITAIN'S OFFICIAL MONSTER RAVING LOONY PARTY** for three years, the only cat to ever lead a political party. One party goal: cat-crossings at all major roads.

DR. JEKYLL was a fluffy ginger cat who made a run for the White House in 2016. **LIMBERBUTT MCCUBBINS**, a Demo-cat, also ran in the same year, with a platform that included low-cost healthcare for pets. His catchy hashtag was **#MEOWISTHETIME**.

EARL GREY ran for Canadian prime minister as leader of the Tuxedo Party in 2015. His main cause was animal cruelty. He was a bit shyer that his late brother, Tuxedo Stan, but a whiff of catnip did wonders.

HANK ran for the United States Senate in 2012 with the slogan **"VOTE THE HUMANS OUT."** His causes included animal rescue and spay and neuter programs. There's a documentary about his campaign called *Wild About Hank*.

MORRIS THE CANDIGATO (cat candidate) launched a social media campaign to become Mayor of Xalapa, Mexico. His slogan was **"TIRED OF VOTING FOR RATS? VOTE FOR A CAT!"** He lost but did better than three of the human candidates.

TUXEDO STAN ran for mayor in Halifax, Canada, in 2012. His **TUXEDO PARTY** platform aimed to raise awareness about the city's booming stray cat population. His campaign became international news, but unfortunately animals in Halifax are banned from holding office.

TURN THE PAGE TO LEARN ABOUT THE ULTIMATE CATS IN CHARGE—FELINES IN ANCIENT EGYPT!

WHEN CATS WERE GODS

Cats were very important in Egypt's harsh desert environment. They killed rats and mice that damaged grain and chased away deadly snakes and scorpions. Without cats, modern civilization might not be the way it is today. Here are some facts about the cool cats of the ancient Egyptian era:

The ancient Egyptians thought of cats as **SACRED ANIMALS** with **MAGICAL POWERS**. They believed having a cat would protect their homes, bring them luck, and heal the sick.

The Egyptians had many gods and goddesses. One of the best known was the **CAT GODDESS BASTET**. She was kind and gentle, with a woman's body and a cat's head. Many believed that cats were descendants of Bastet and should be treated like royalty.

Cats were such a part of Egyptian life that families would go into mourning whenever their pet kitty died. They even **SHAVED OFF THEIR EYEBROWS** to show their grief!

The Egyptians adored cats so much that their lives were considered **EQUAL TO HUMANS' LIVES**. Anyone who killed a cat, even by accident, was punished with **DEATH**.

The Egyptian word for *cat*—*MAU*—sounds like the mew of an actual cat.

EGYPTIAN AMULETS featuring an image of a cat and her kittens were often worn by women who wanted to have a child.

The Egyptian sun god, Ra, was said to **TURN HIMSELF INTO A CAT** each night in order to fight the evil serpent Apopis.

The ancient Egyptians worshipped the sun and feared the darkness, so they were fascinated and awed by the cat's apparent ability to see in the dark.

It was strictly forbidden to export Egypt's precious cats, but **TRADERS** and **SMUGGLERS** managed to sneak them out anyway.

Images of cats **DECKED OUT IN JEWELS** can be found in ancient Egyptian paintings, jewelry, and sculptures. Cats were rarely portrayed in a sleeping position—only sitting up—as this was considered a show of respect.

The first cat **TO HAVE A NAME** (that we know of) was **BOUHAKI**, a cat who appears in Egyptian carvings that date back to around 1950 BC.

CAT FACT
Mummification was very important to the ancient Egyptians. They believed that if their bodies survived they could become immortal. Cats were mummified, too! A cat mummy could be used as a temple offering, buried in a mass grave, or placed in a tomb alongside its owner. Some grief-stricken owners even included some yummy mummy mice for their kitty's journey to the afterlife.

TAMA
JAPAN'S FURRIEST STATIONMASTER

The Japanese people believe that being kind to cats brings good luck. That's definitely true for a kitty named Tama, who changed the fortunes of a big company.

Tama grew up near the Kishi train station in the Japanese countryside. People often stopped to give her a snack or a cuddle. But even though Tama was popular, the station wasn't. So few used it that the railway company thought about closing it for good—until someone had a wacky idea. Why not make Tama the stationmaster!

A feline stationmaster in cat-crazy Japan? It turned out to be a genius idea. Proudly wearing her custom-made cap and badge, Tama greeted passengers and posed for photos. People started coming to the station just to see the cute kitty at work. So many came that they filled up all the trains. It saved the railway company from going bust.

Tama was swiftly promoted to Ultra Stationmaster. She had her own office with a litter box, two kitty assistants, and a salary paid in food. She also became a vice president of the railway. That made her the company's top-ranking female employee (and the only one with fur).

Tama's fame grew and grew, especially after she appeared in two documentaries and a TV show. She became such a star that they made a "Tama Train" with cat-shaped seats and Tama cartoons! Kishi Station was rebuilt to look like a cat's face and has a café and shop selling Tama-themed gifts.

Tama paved the way for other animal stationmasters, including cats, dogs, goats, a pair of monkeys, and—for one day only—even a penguin!

1999–2015
JAPAN

CAT CRAZY IN JAPAN

Japan is a country that's nuts about cats. How nuts, you might ask? When stationmaster **TAMA** passed away after eight years on the job, she was declared a **SHINTO GODDESS**. She was also given a fantastic new job title: **HONORABLE ETERNAL STATIONMASTER!**

Take a walk just about anywhere in Japan and you'll see cat faces on nearly every product imaginable. You can also visit cat cafés, dress up in feline-themed fashion, and even eat cat-shaped pizzas, cakes, and pasta.

What's with the kitty obsession? One reason is that in Japanese folklore, cats have special powers and are a symbol of **GOOD FORTUNE**. Another reason is that cats are cute, and in Japan, cuteness is a highly coveted quality.

HERE ARE SOME MORE THINGS FOR CAT LOVERS TO LOOK FOR IN JAPAN:

GOTOKUJI TEMPLE in Tokyo is the famous birthplace of the **MANEKI NEKO** (Beckoning Cat) good luck charm. Legend has it that during a bad storm, a temple cat waved her paw to invite a feudal lord inside and saved him from harm. Today, there are thousands of **LUCKY CAT** figurines on display there.

Tokyo has more than a **HUNDRED CAT CAFÉS** where people sip lattes and play with cute kitties. There's even a cat café train, filled with felines that are up for adoption.

A pilgrimage to the **HELLO KITTY THEME PARK** in Tokyo is a must for any fan of the cute cat-like cartoon. More than 1.5 million people come here each year to enjoy shows and rides and to peek inside a life-size replica of Hello Kitty's house.

There are more pussycats than people on Tashirojima, one of a dozen or so **CAT ISLANDS** off the main island of Japan.

At **GOTANJOJI TEMPLE**—also known as Kitty Temple—dozens of homeless cats are cared for by **BUDDHIST MONKS**. Visitors can get a special kitty fortune to see what's in store for the coming year.

The Japanese celebrate **NYAN NYAN NYAN DAY** every February 22. The Japanese word for *two* sounds like the Japanese word for *meow*. That means the date 2/22 is pronounced *nyan nyan nyan* (**MEOW MEOW MEOW**). A *purr*-fect day for Cat Day! It's a fun excuse to post photos and videos of adorable felines on social media.

JAPANESE ANIMATION is chock-full with cats. The whimsical animated tale *Kiki's Delivery Service* features a witch and a sarcastic black cat named **JIJI**. Another animated film, *The Cat Returns*, stars a young girl with the dreamy ability to speak to cats. There are also lots of cats in Japanese comic books (**MANGA**) and advertisements.

TOWSER
THE WORLD'S DEADLIEST DISTILLERY CAT

A bronze statue of a cat stands in a place of honor at Glenturret, which claims to be the oldest whisky distillery in Scotland. Towser is considered to be the greatest mouser of all time.

Cats have been on rodent patrol at distilleries for centuries. It takes a lot of grain to make whisky, and where there's grain there are mice. As a mouser, Towser was in a league of her own. She earned herself a Guinness World Record as the World Mousing Champion, credited with 28,899 kills.

28,899 kills . . . how did they came up with that mind-boggling number? Did Towser lay out her victims each morning to be counted?

What happened was that a team from Guinness World Records heard about Towser and came to see the natural-born assassin in action. They guesstimated that she killed three mice a day every day of her adult life. No other cat has ever come close to beating her record. And probably never will.

What was the secret of Towser's success? There are whispers that it might have something to do with the "wee dram" of whisky added to her saucer of milk each night. More likely, she just loved the thrill of the chase.

For nearly twenty-four years, Towser's reign as Glenturret's head of rodent patrol made her a celebrity, with TV appearances and photos with her fans. Nowadays, it's more important for a distillery cat to be cute and charming than to be a good hunter. It's enough to send Towser spinning in her grave, but at least she can rest assured she will forever be the world's number-one mouser.

1963–1987
SCOTLAND

CAUTION: CATS AT WORK

There have been a lot of **HARD-WORKING CATS** with jobs over the years, just like **TOWSER** the champion mouser!

TAKE A LOOK AT SOME OF THESE WORKER CATS:

Radio-station cat **FEEDBACK** was a mouser at WJCO Radio in Jackson, Michigan. He also greeted visitors and even went into the studio at times to add a feline spin to the broadcast.

Crosswalk patrol cat **SABLE** was proud to wear his official orange jacket and took his job very seriously (no jokes about black cats crossing roads, please). He kept little kids safe!

TV star **JASON** was a Siamese cat who was the first in a long line of presenter pussycats on *Blue Peter,* a popular children's television program in Britain.

Museum cat **MIKE** guarded the gate of the British Museum in London for twenty years.

Bicycle courier **MJ** makes her rounds on her human's shoulders.

Fire-station cat **FLAME** is a great companion for firefighters and helps them relax and de-stress after battling a dangerous blaze. Flame was named ASPCA (American Society for the Prevention of Cruelty to Animals) Cat of the Year 2017.

FRED the "Undercover Kitty" helped the New York Police Department bust a man who was impersonating a veterinarian.

Assistant librarian **KUZYA** loves bow ties and works at a library in Russia. The place has been busier since he arrived. People come to see him but stay for the books.

BROTHER CREAM ran his own convenience store in Hong Kong. He became a local celebrity after he was allegedly cat-napped in 2012 and found twenty-six days later in an alleyway. The incident made front page news and a biography was written about him.

In 2001, **CC (COPY CAT)** was the world's first cloned pet. Her job was to serve as a sort of living science experiment as scientists watched her grow up. Aside from her history-making birth, she was a perfectly ordinary cat who had kittens the old-fashioned way.

The CIA launched a top-secret project to spy on the Russians in the 1960s. The plan was to train cats to eavesdrop on conversations. **THE FIRST FELINE AGENT** had a microphone in his ear, a transmitter near his collar, and an antenna in his tail. No cats were ever used and the project was scrapped.

DID YOU KNOW?
A BELGIAN VILLAGE ONCE TRAINED CATS TO DELIVER MAIL. THE PLAN WAS TO TAKE ADVANTAGE OF THE CATS' RENOWNED HOMING INSTINCTS, CARRYING LETTERS IN BAGS AROUND THEIR NECKS. TO THE RELIEF OF HUMAN MAIL CARRIERS, THE PLAN WAS A CAT-ASTROPHE.

TRIM
AUSSIE ADVENTURER ON THE HIGH SEAS

Centuries ago, most people thought Australia was a collection of islands. But not Captain Matthew Flinders—he was sure it was a continent. He was the first to map Australia's coastline, but he didn't do it alone. He was helped by his cat, Trim.

Trim was born at sea. He fell overboard once as a kitten but climbed a rope to safety. He had great balance, no fear of water, and kept the crew amused by performing new tricks. The captain made notes in his logbook about the funny things Trim did. At dinnertime, for example, the cat would tap each man with his paw. If Trim didn't get a tasty morsel to eat, he'd snatch a bite right off their forks!

Whenever Trim was on solid ground, he longed to be back on the water. On the captain's third South Pacific voyage, Trim spent several years at Flinders's side as they sailed all the way around Australia. There was no place he'd rather be.

On the way back to England, the ship crashed into a coral reef. The captain, Trim, and the other survivors swam to a nearby island, where Trim kept them entertained until they were rescued two months later. But their bad luck wasn't over. When the ship stopped for repairs on the island of Mauritius, the captain was accused of spying and held prisoner for six years!

The loyal kitty stayed with Captain Flinders until one day he disappeared, never to be seen again. The heartbroken captain described Trim as one of the finest animals he ever knew. Statues stand in his honor in England and Australia, showing that his legend lives on.

1797–1803
AUSTRALIA

A CAT-LOVER'S GUIDE TO WORLD TRAVEL

Do **TRIM'S** adventures inspire you to travel the world? Here are some places for cat lovers to go and see!

FESTIVAL OF THE CATS, YPRES, BELGIUM
At Belgium's annual *Kattenstoet,* people dressed as kitties parade down the streets and toy cats are tossed from the belfry.

ERNEST HEMINGWAY HOME AND MUSEUM, KEY WEST, FLORIDA
Dozens of six-toed cats roam around the author's former home like they own the place.

TORRE ARGENTINA CAT SANCTUARY, ROME, ITALY
Visitors can volunteer at this outdoor sanctuary, where stray cats live among ancient ruins.

THE CATBOAT, AMSTERDAM, THE NETHERLANDS
The world's most famous cat sanctuary is on a houseboat named *Poezenboot*. It's a top tourist attraction.

LE CAFÉ DES CHATS, PARIS, FRANCE
All the kitties at this charming locale were homeless once upon a time. As one might expect in France, the focus is on the expertly prepared food as much as the felines.

LUCKY CAT TRAIL, YORK, ENGLAND
York has warded off evil spirits for centuries with rooftop cat statues across the city.

CHARTWELL, KENT, ENGLAND
Winston Churchill loved his ginger cat so much, he wrote a will requesting that Jock be allowed to spend the rest of his days at the former prime minister's country home. In fact, he asked that there always be a ginger cat with a white bib and four white socks in residence at Chartwell. The house is currently home to Jock VI.

ISTANBUL, TURKEY
Turkey's largest city has long been a haven for stray cats that are cared for by locals. Cat-loving travelers can stay at the cat-themed Stray Cat Hostel, which welcomes feline strays as well as humans.

MYKONOS, GREECE
This island is famous for its cats, which prowl the postcard-perfect cobblestone streets.

THE VILLAGE OF CIORANI, ROMANIA
With four cats to each human, this hamlet has been named the "World Capital of Cats."

LADY DINAH'S CAT EMPORIUM, LONDON, ENGLAND
Head here for cake and a *purr*-fect cup of tea surrounded by friendly rescue cats.

KUCHING, MALAYSIA
The world's first cat-themed city is filled with feline statues, public art, and museums.

JUST ABOUT ANYWHERE IN JAPAN
The country has all sorts of cat cafés, cat temples, cat islands, cat everything. Just go!

TRIXIE
TOWER OF LONDON PRISONER

One of the spookiest buildings in England is the Tower of London. It was used as a prison for many centuries, and there was a time when nothing was more terrifying than being sent to the Tower.

One Tower prisoner was Henry Wriothesley, who was busted for plotting against Queen Elizabeth I. He was a lord, but that didn't make life behind bars much easier. He was sick, lonely, and down in the dumps. Imagine the look on Lord Henry's face when his favorite cat, Trixie, appeared out of nowhere!

How did Trixie manage to find her way to her owner's cell? Some say she crept over rooftops, scaled the Tower walls, and climbed down through the unlit chimney. A more likely story is that Lord Henry's wife smuggled the cat in during a visit. It may always be a mystery. What is known, though, is that Trixie kept Lord Henry company during his long and dreary imprisonment.

Lord Henry's love for Trixie was just as remarkable. At a time when felines were linked to witchcraft, few would dare to admit they even liked cats, let alone be devoted to one as much as he was. Yet the nobleman loved his furry friend so much that he hired an artist to paint their portrait.

This was no ordinary painting, though. As well as showcasing the pair's bond, it also contained clever clues that suggested Lord Henry was a fan of the newly crowned monarch, James I. In 1603, he sent the painting to the king with a plan to help himself get freed—and it worked!

But was he freed because of the secret messages? Or did the king decide that any man with such a loyal pet couldn't be all that bad? Either way, James I freed Lord Henry (and Trixie, too) and they both went on to bigger and better things.

1601–UNKNOWN
ENGLAND

THE HEALING POWERS OF CATS

Cats like **TRIXIE** can do more than boost someone's spirits. People have long suspected that cats have the power to **HEAL**. There is even some scientific evidence to prove it!

Some felines can be **NATURAL "DOCTORS"** with a sixth sense for when their humans are feeling under the weather. They might offer comfort and support if they sense you need it.

When people think of therapy animals, they usually think of dogs or maybe horses. But **THERAPY CATS** are being used more and more in retirement homes, nursing homes, schools, hospices, and other healthcare facilities.

CAT FACT
A good therapy cat must be **FRIENDLY**, **PATIENT**, **CONFIDENT**, **GENTLE**, and **AT EASE** in any situation. They must enjoy contact with adults as well as children and tolerate being pet and sometimes handled in a clumsy manner by different people. They must also adapt easily to the sight and sounds of medical equipment, wheelchairs, and unfamiliar noises in a hospital or home environment.

Life is less **LONELY** with a cat. Cats make perfect companions for people who live alone. They're especially great for older people—there's even some evidence showing that elderly people with cats live longer and healthier lives than those who don't have them.

Petting a cat's fur is said to be able to put the mind at ease and clear negative thoughts, which really helps people with **DEPRESSION** and **ANXIETY**.

THE POWER OF PURRS

The steady sound of a **CAT'S PURR** can ease the pain of a bad headache. A purring cat also creates vibrations that—believe it or not—can actually help strengthen bones and repair damage to muscles, ligaments, and tendons. Animal doctors have known this for generations. In fact, according to an old veterinary adage, "If you put a cat in a room with a bunch of broken bones, the bones will heal."

HOW DOES IT WORK?

When the body does high-intensity exercise and strength training, bones and muscles become **STRONGER**. A cat's purr works in much the same way, except that it uses low-frequency vibrations instead of high-impact activity.

INCREDIBLE (BUT TRUE) CAT FACTS

1. House cats are the only cat species that can hold their tail vertically while walking.

2. Cats see the world in shades of green and blue.

3. A cat's heart beats almost twice as fast as a human's—about 120–140 beats a minute.

4. Cats have 473 taste buds. Humans have 9,000.

5. A cat cannot see directly under its nose.

6. Dogs need to be house-trained, but most cats use the litter box with little training. It's a cat's natural instinct to cover its waste.

7. Cat urine glows under ultraviolet light.

8. A cat in a tree can only go down backward, not headfirst.

9. Cat fur is 95 percent protein.

10. Hairballs the size of baseballs have been removed from the stomachs of cats.

11. Many pure white cats with blue eyes are deaf.

12. When a cat holds its tail high in the air, it means it is happy.

13. It's more dangerous for cats to fall from a low height than from a high one.

14. Most cats snooze between 12 and 16 hours each day. That can be about 70 percent of their lifetime!

15. Cats usually live for about 12 to 15 years. Some cats have been known to live twice that long.

16. Calico cats are almost always female. Ditto for tortoiseshell cats.

17. Napoleon, Julius Caesar, and Charles XI were all ruthless rulers who were afraid of cats.

18. Cats can make approximately 100 different sounds.

19. Many cats are lactose intolerant (so don't give them any cow's milk!).

20. Chocolate and lilies can both be harmful to cats.

21. There's no such thing as a vegetarian kitty. Cats need to eat meat to survive.

22. A group of cats is called a clowder.

23. Cats purr when they're happy but also when they are hungry, scared, or injured.

24. Adult cats meow only to communicate with humans.

25. Cats can "taste" smells, thanks to a special organ in the roof of their mouth.

FEARLESS FELINES TIMELINE

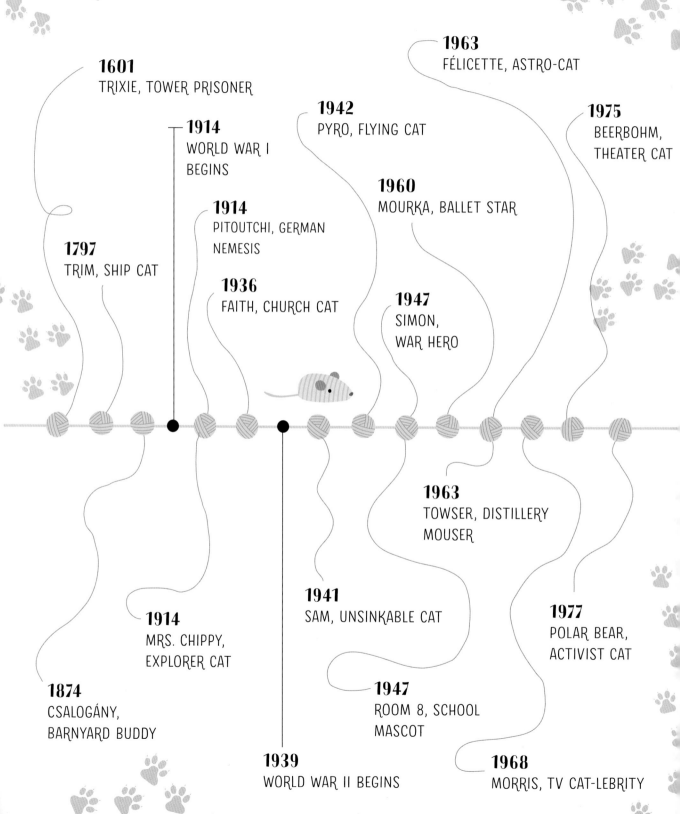

1601
TRIXIE, TOWER PRISONER

1914
WORLD WAR I
BEGINS

1942
PYRO, FLYING CAT

1963
FÉLICETTE, ASTRO-CAT

1975
BEERBOHM,
THEATER CAT

1914
PITOUTCHI, GERMAN
NEMESIS

1960
MOURKA, BALLET STAR

1797
TRIM, SHIP CAT

1936
FAITH, CHURCH CAT

1947
SIMON,
WAR HERO

1963
TOWSER, DISTILLERY
MOUSER

1914
MRS. CHIPPY,
EXPLORER CAT

1941
SAM, UNSINKABLE CAT

1977
POLAR BEAR,
ACTIVIST CAT

1874
CSALOGÁNY,
BARNYARD BUDDY

1947
ROOM 8, SCHOOL
MASCOT

1939
WORLD WAR II BEGINS

1968
MORRIS, TV CAT-LEBRITY

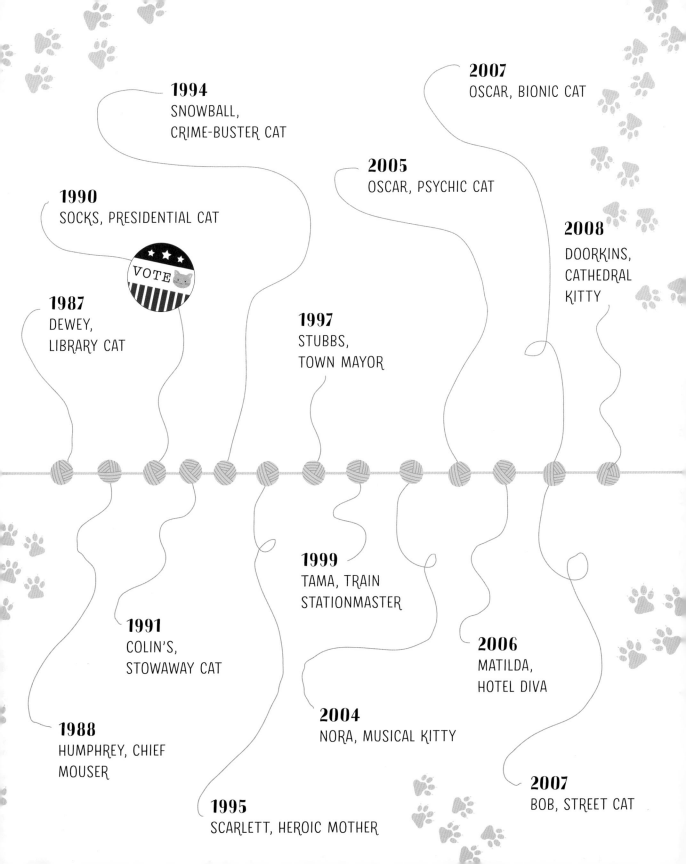

1994
SNOWBALL,
CRIME-BUSTER CAT

2007
OSCAR, BIONIC CAT

1990
SOCKS, PRESIDENTIAL CAT

2005
OSCAR, PSYCHIC CAT

2008
DOORKINS,
CATHEDRAL
KITTY

VOTE

1987
DEWEY,
LIBRARY CAT

1997
STUBBS,
TOWN MAYOR

1999
TAMA, TRAIN
STATIONMASTER

1991
COLIN'S,
STOWAWAY CAT

2006
MATILDA,
HOTEL DIVA

1988
HUMPHREY, CHIEF
MOUSER

2004
NORA, MUSICAL KITTY

2007
BOB, STREET CAT

1995
SCARLETT, HEROIC MOTHER

GLOSSARY

AIRSHIP — An aircraft that is kept aloft with a gas that is lighter than air, such as helium.

ALLIES — The victorious Allied nations of World War I and II, including Britain, France, Italy, Russia, and the United States.

AMULET — An ornament or small piece of jewelry thought to give protection against evil, danger, or disease.

ASAP — Short for "as soon as possible."

BEERBOHM — Beerbohm the cat was named after Sir Herbert Beerbohm Tree, an English actor and theater manager who lived in the late 1800s/early 1900s.

BLACK DEATH — Also known as the bubonic plague, a terrible disease that hit Britain and Europe in 1348 and killed millions of people.

BREEDER — Someone who breeds animals, such as purebred cats. An example of a purebred is a cat whose parents were both Siamese.

CALICO — Calicos are usually female cats with orange (ginger), black, and white fur.

CATNIP — An herb belonging to the mint family.

CIVIL WAR — A war between citizens of the same country.

CLARK GABLE — An American actor referred to as "The King of Hollywood."

CLONE — A living thing that is genetically the same as another living thing.

CREPUSCULAR — Describes an animal that is mostly active at dawn and dusk.

DEWEY DECIMAL SYSTEM — A system used in libraries to classify books and other publications.

DIABETIC — A person with diabetes, a disease that occurs when the body can't use glucose (a type of sugar) normally.

DNA — DNA is in every cell of the body. It's the material that carries all the information about how a living thing will look and act.

DOMESTIC CAT/HOUSE CAT — A tame cat that lives among humans and is kept as a pet.

ENTREPURR-NEUR — A cat that goes into business, from *entrepreneur*.

FERAL CAT — A cat that was born and lives outdoors with little or no human contact. Also known as street cats, homeless cats, and community cats.

FORENSIC SCIENCE — Using scientific methods to solve crimes.

GANGPLANK — A moveable plank used by passengers to board or disembark from a ship or boat.

HMS — Short for "His/Her Majesty's Ship."

KIWI — A nickname for someone from New Zealand.

LITERARY AGENT — Someone who negotiates publishing deals on behalf of an author.

MAINE COON — A large, friendly, long-haired cat, often referred to as a "gentle giant."

MICROCHIP — A tiny computer chip placed under a cat's skin. It has info about the cat in case it gets lost.

MYTHOLOGY — A collection of myths (stories) that explain the mysteries of life.

NAZIS — Members of a fascist political party led by Adolf Hitler from 1933 to 1945.

NEMESIS — A person or thing (or cat!) that is difficult to defeat.

NEUTER — Surgery that means a male cat can't father any kittens.

PERSIAN — A long-haired cat with a rather round head, stocky body, and short, thick legs.

RAF — Short for "Royal Air Force."

RAGDOLL — A breed of cat known for its friendly and laid-back personality, silky fur, and beautiful blue eyes. They love people and may be called "ragdolls" because they like to be carried around!

RMS — Short for "Royal Mail Ship."

SHELTER — A place that offers temporary housing and protection, such as an animal shelter.

SIEGE — A military action that involves surrounding a town or building and cutting off essential supplies, with the aim of forcing those inside to surrender.

SIXTH SENSE — An ability to know something without using any of the five senses (sight, hearing, touch, smell, or taste). Also described as having a "hunch" or a "gut feeling."

SPAY — Surgery that means a female cat can't have any kittens.

SPHYNX — A breed of cat that doesn't have any fur. They look a bit alien-like!

STRAY — A tame cat with no home or owner, not the same as a feral cat.

SUPERSTITION — An irrational belief. There are lots of superstitions about cats, especially black ones.

TABBY — A tabby isn't a breed of cat, it's a coat pattern. It can be striped, swirly, or spotted. Many tabbies also have a mark that looks like an *M* on their forehead.

TANKER — A cargo ship with tanks designed to carry liquids (such as oil) in large quantities.

TOMCAT — A male cat that hasn't been neutered.

TORTOISESHELL — A "tortie" is usually a female cat with a mix of orange and black fur.

TUXEDO CAT — A cat that is black with a white bib and paws. It often has a white belly, too.

VIP — Short for "very important person."

WHY ARE CATS SO WEIRD?
QUIZ ANSWERS

1. WHY DO CATS LIKE BOXES?
A: THEY'RE A SAFE HIDING PLACE

Cats like places that make them feel protected, especially when they can see out. This explains why cats LOVE boxes with a few holes cut out of them.

2. WHY DO CATS HATE GETTING WET?
A: NOT ALL CATS DO

Wet, heavy fur makes some cats uncomfortable. It can make them feel chilly, too. But many cats don't mind water at all. Some even like to go swimming!

3. WHY DO CATS LIKE HIGH PLACES?
C: BOTH — THEY FEEL SAFER AND WARMER THERE

A high perch makes cats feel safer. They can see what's going on and they're out of reach of dogs and other dangers. It's also warmer up there, because heat rises.

4. WHY DO CATS USE A LITTER BOX?
B: IT'S INSTINCT

Cats in the wild cover their waste without any training. They do it to hide the scent from their predators. House cats do it for exactly the same reason!

5. WHAT ARE THE "ZOOMIES"?
A: WHEN A CAT RUNS AROUND FOR NO APPARENT REASON

Ever seen a cat suddenly bolt from one room to another, or race around like a fool? You've witnessed a classic case of the "zoomies." Most times there is no reason for it whatsoever. It's a fun and harmless way to unleash pent-up energy.

6. WHY DO CATS GO A BIT CRAZY AROUND CATNIP?
C: NO ONE REALLY KNOWS

Some cats find the smell of catnip irresistible. Other cats don't give a hoot about it. Scientists aren't quite sure how catnip works on cats or why it lasts only a short time.

7. WHY DO CATS GROOM THEMSELVES SO MUCH?
B: ALL KINDS OF REASONS

Cats spend an astonishing amount of time grooming themselves—about half their waking hours! Aside from cleanliness, cats groom themselves to distribute natural oils through their coat and to cool down by dampening their fur with saliva. It's also very relaxing and a way to "self soothe" in a stressful situation.

8. WHY ARE HOUSE CATS MOST ACTIVE AT DAWN AND DUSK?
B: THEY ARE CREPUSCULAR

Crepuscular simply means an animal is mainly active during twilight hours. Most house cats fall into this category, although many cats adapt their activity levels so that they're more in sync with their human caregivers.

FURR-THER READING

Are you a curious-as-a-cat reader? Here are some books that offer additional details about various Fearless Felines. There are also a handful of cat-centric websites on the next page.

BOOKS

A STREET CAT NAMED BOB — James Bowen

DEWEY: THE SMALL-TOWN LIBRARY CAT WHO TOUCHED THE WORLD — Vicki Myron

DOORKINS THE CATHEDRAL CAT — Lisa Gutwein

TWO PERFECTLY MARVELOUS CATS — Rosamond M. Young

A DAY IN THE LIFE OF HUMPHREY THE DOWNING STREET CAT — David Brawn

MATILDA, THE ALGONQUIN CAT — Leslie Martini

MRS. CHIPPY'S LAST EXPEDITION — Caroline Alexander

MAKING ROUNDS WITH OSCAR: THE EXTRAORDINARY GIFT OF AN ORDINARY CAT — David Dosa

OSCAR: THE BIONIC CAT — Kate Allan

THE CAT WHO CAME FOR CHRISTMAS — Cleveland Amory

SCARLETT SAVES HER FAMILY — Jane Martin and Jean-Claude Suarès

ABLE SEACAT SIMON — Lynne Barrett-Lee

DEAR SOCKS, DEAR BUDDY — Hillary Rodham Clinton

TRIM: THE STORY OF A BRAVE, SEAFARING CAT — Matthew Flinders

WEBSITES

ASPCA.ORG
The official website for the American Society for the Prevention of Cruelty to Animals.

CATHEDRAL.SOUTHWARK.ANGLICAN.ORG/VISITING/DOORKINS-MAGNIFICAT/
A website dedicated to Doorkins, Magnificat.

CATS.ORG.UK
The official website for Cats Protection, the UK's top feline welfare charity, has adoption stories, helpful information about cat care, and the *Meow!* blog.

CATSTER.COM
Catster compiles helpful (and often hilarious) information for cat lovers.

IHEARTCATS.COM
This site offers news and information about cats, as well as fun and unique products that support animal shelters and rescue organizations.

KATZENWORLD.CO.UK
Katzenworld has lots of cute stories about cats, as well as more serious articles about cat health and advice, product reviews, and competitions.

LOVEMEOW.COM
Love Meow features inspiring and heartwarming stories about cats, cat rescues, and cat foster parents from all over the world.

NORATHEPIANOCAT.COM/CATCERTO
A wesbite dedicated to Nora, the piano cat.

RSPCA.ORG.UK
The official website for the Royal Society for the Prevention of Cruelty to Animals.

STREETCATBOB.WORLD
A website dedicated to Street Cat Bob.

TOP TIP
Always stay safe and be cautious online. Every effort has been taken to ensure the information held on these websites is appropriate at the time of publication, but Scholastic is not responsible for the content on third-party websites.

ABOUT THE AUTHOR

KIMBERLIE HAMILTON is a writer who used to live in sunny Southern California and now lives in misty northern Scotland with her fiancé, John, and four cats. She has written all sorts of things over the years, including travel brochures, screenplays, websites, and teaching materials for her English students in Japan. She is passionate about animals (especially cats!) and loves to write entertaining nonfiction books for children. Kimberlie has a master's degree in screenwriting from the University of California, Los Angeles, and is currently pursuing another master's in Creative and Cultural Communication at the University of Aberdeen. She shares her latest adventures and photos in her travel and lifestyle blog, *The Hippie Chick's Guide to the Highlands*.

KIMBERLIEHAMILTON.CO.UK

Kimberlie wishes to thank her devoted feline companions, Scout and Sammy Jo, who served as the inspiration for this book (and many other things).

SCOUT
Author's Assistant

SAMMY JO
Creative Advisor

ABOUT THE ILLUSTRATORS

ALLIE RUNNION

Allie is a designer and illustrator. She graduated from the Rhode Island School of Design with a degree in Illustration and English, and has worked for several companies, both on a full-time and freelance basis. Illustrations: **DEWEY** and **STUBBS**.

ANDREW GARDNER

Andrew grew up with four cats and is a lifetime doodler, drawing since childhood. After a decade of working as a designer and art director, he decided to pursue his passion for illustration and storytelling. Illustrations: **MRS. CHIPPY** and **TOWSER**.

BECKY DAVIES

Becky is a British illustrator currently living and working in the beautiful town of Chepstow, Wales, with her partner. She graduated from the University of Gloucestershire with a First Class BA (Hons) in Illustration. Illustrations: **MATILDA** and **SIMON**.

CHARLOTTE ARCHER

Fortunate enough to secure a job with a lovely greeting card company at the age of eighteen, Charlotte became a self-taught illustrator and designer. More than fifteen years on, she is delighted to be working as a firmly established, full-time freelance illustrator. Illustrations: various images throughout.

EMMA JAYNE

Emma Jayne is an illustrator from the beautiful county of Cheshire, in the North West of England. She likes to work both digitally and traditionally, usually starting off by painting with gouache, using ink and colored pencils, then finishing off in Photoshop. Illustrations: **SCARLETT** and **HUMPHREY**.

HOLLY STERLING

Holly is a a freelance children's author and illustrator based in the North East of England. She loves to work by hand using a variety of different media including watercolor, pencil, and different printing processes. Illustrations: **FAITH** and **NORA**.

HUI SKIPP

Born and raised in Taiwan, Hui graduated with a Sculpture and Fine Art degree. Hui is passionate about animals, from tiny termites to giant humpback whales dancing in the Pacific Ocean. Illustrations: **MORRIS** and **PYRO**.

JESSICA SMITH

Jessica is a graduate from Falmouth University and is currently living in a small town near Oxford, England. She enjoys working conceptually, so scale and perspective play a large role within the images that she makes. Illustrations: **COLIN'S** and **ROOM 8**.

KATIE WILSON

Katie lives and works in an old railway house in the beautiful South Island of New Zealand. She creates for both adults and children, and her illustrations are sweet and cheerful with a handmade feel. Illustrations: **DOORKINS** and **TRIM**.

LILY ROSSITER

Lily is an illustrator, ceramicist, and all-time lover of patterns and picture books. Her work is naïve and quirky with a charming, playful twist. Illustrations: **CSALOGÁNY** and **SNOWBALL**.

MICHELLE HIRD

Michelle is an author, illustrator, and graphic designer. Her work has been showcased on numerous editorial pieces. Michelle was nominated for the International Content Marketing Award in 2015 for an editorial piece she did for *Completely London*. Illustrations: **FÉLICETTE** and **OSCAR**.

NAN LAWSON

Nan is a glasses-wearing, coffee-drinking illustrator based in Los Angeles. There, she lives with her husband, daughter, and two chubby cats. She has had clients in both the publishing world and television industry. Illustrations: **MOURKA** and **PITOUTCHI**.

OLIVIA HOLDEN

Olivia was born and raised in a small village in Lancashire. Following her degree, Olivia continued to develop her love for print and illustration, creating her own work for textiles, books, and stationery. Illustrations: **BOB** and **OSCAR**.

RACHEL ALLSOP

Rachel works from a little studio in her home in Lancashire, England. She finds inspiration in nature and loves to include plants and animals in her illustrations. She spent her early years living in Japan, and the culture continues to influence her work today. Colors make her happy—the brighter the better! Illustrations: **POLAR BEAR** and **TAMA**.

RACHEL SANSON

Rachel is an illustrator from the north of England. She graduated from the University of Lincoln with a degree in Illustration after studying for three years in a little studio perched on top of a hill. Illustrations: **SAM** and **TRIXIE**.

BONNIE PANG

Bonnie is an illustrator from Hong Kong. She holds a Master's degree in Illustration from The Academy of Art University. Her experience includes concept art for animation studios, children's book illustration, commercial illustration and public art projects. Illustrations: cover.

SAM LOMAN

Sam studied Illustration at the Williem de Kooning Academy in Rotterdam in 2005 and Art and Design at University of Hertfordshire in 2011. She runs her own design business, which includes illustration, graphic design, photography, product design, and writing children's books. Illustrations: **BEERBOHM** and **SOCKS**.

INDEX